Being Brahmin: The Ancestral Flames

Vipresh Dwivedi

DEDICATION

This book is dedicated to all those who seek to understand the multifaceted role of Brahmins in society. To the scholars, thinkers, and leaders who have tirelessly contributed to the advancement of knowledge and wisdom. To the individuals who have embraced inclusivity, acceptance, and social justice. To the cultural custodians who have preserved and propagated India's rich heritage. And to the future generations who will carry forward the legacy of Brahmin contributions with integrity and compassion.

May this book serve as a tribute to the resilience, intellect, and cultural richness of the Brahmin community. May it inspire dialogue, foster understanding, and promote harmony in a world that thrives on diversity and mutual respect.

ACKNOWLEDGEMENT

I would like to express my sincere gratitude to my esteemed teachers, Sudha Bajpai and Sarita Shukla, whose guidance, wisdom, and encouragement have been invaluable in shaping my understanding of Brahmin culture and society. Their insights, patience, and mentorship have inspired me to delve deeper into this intricate subject matter and to approach it with sensitivity and respect.

I also extend my heartfelt thanks to all those who have contributed to the creation of this book, directly or indirectly, through their support, feedback, and encouragement. Your contributions have enriched the content and enhanced its overall quality.

Furthermore, I wish to emphasize that the views expressed in this book are intended to foster understanding, promote dialogue, and celebrate the diverse perspectives within Brahmin society. It is not the intention of this book to offend or hurt the sentiments of any individual or community. Rather, it is an earnest attempt to shed light on the complexities, contributions, and challenges faced by the Brahmin community in a spirit of empathy and inclusivity.

It's important to note that our discussions about Brahmins in this book are centered around their traditional professions. Over time, however, the notion of being a Brahmin became entrenched in birth rather than profession, a transition that we examine as we progress into modern times.

Once again, I extend my deepest gratitude to all who have played a part in bringing this book to fruition.

PROLOGUE

In the vast tapestry of human history, certain communities have played pivotal roles in shaping the cultural, intellectual, and spiritual landscape of society. Among these communities, the Brahmins of India stand as custodians of ancient wisdom, guardians of tradition, and torchbearers of knowledge.

This book delves into the multifaceted world of Brahmins, exploring their origins, duties, contributions, and challenges across different epochs of history and in the contemporary era. Through meticulous research, insightful analysis, and nuanced storytelling, we embark on a journey to unravel the complexities of Brahmin culture and society.

From the Vedic period to the present day, we trace the evolution of Brahmin identity and examine the roles they have played in shaping diverse facets of society, including politics, education, religion, and the arts. We confront misconceptions, challenge stereotypes, and highlight the rich tapestry of Brahmin contributions to human civilization.

As we navigate through the pages of this book, we encounter stories of resilience, intellectual brilliance, and social activism that characterize the Brahmin ethos. We engage in critical reflections on the challenges faced by Brahmins in an ever-changing world and contemplate their future trajectory amidst globalization, technological advancement, and social transformation.

Above all, this book is a testament to the enduring legacy of Brahmins, whose quest for knowledge, commitment to service, and pursuit of spiritual enlightenment continue to inspire and enrich humanity. It is an invitation to explore, understand, and appreciate the profound and multifaceted role of Brahmins in shaping the world we inhabit today.

Contents

PREFACE

The Brahmin community has long been a subject of fascination, admiration, and at times, controversy. As a community deeply intertwined with the fabric of Indian society, Brahmins have left an indelible mark on history, culture, and intellectual thought. Yet, amidst the reverence and scrutiny, the true essence of Brahmin identity often remains shrouded in misconceptions and stereotypes.

This book seeks to unravel the layers of complexity surrounding Brahmin culture and society, offering a comprehensive exploration of their origins, traditions, contributions, and challenges. Drawing upon historical records, scholarly research, and personal narratives, we embark on a journey to uncover the rich tapestry of

Brahmin heritage.

From the ancient Vedic scriptures to the modern era, each chapter delves into different aspects of Brahmin life, shedding light on their roles as intellectuals, educators, spiritual guides, and societal leaders. We confront prevalent stereotypes and myths, while also acknowledging the nuances and diversity within the Brahmin community.

Throughout these pages, we aim not only to inform but also to inspire dialogue, reflection, and understanding. Our goal is to foster a deeper appreciation for Brahmin culture and to encourage readers to critically engage with the complexities of caste, identity, and social dynamics in contemporary India.

It is my hope that this book serves as a catalyst for meaningful conversations, challenging preconceptions, and promoting inclusivity and acceptance. By shedding light on the multifaceted world of Brahmins, we embark on a journey of discovery, empathy, and mutual respect.

Chapter 1: Introduction to Brahmins

Before delving into discussions surrounding Brahmins and casteism, it is imperative to embark on a broader exploration of their historical roots. The term "casteism" found its way into the Indian lexicon during the British colonial era, courtesy of Herbert Hope Risley. However, its precursor, "Jaati," denoting social and professional groupings, had existed in a milder form within Indian society. The British, through their classification efforts, not only institutionalized caste but also exacerbated existing social divisions, deepening the fault lines within Indian society.

The original concept, "Jaati," is noted to have been a subtle aspect of the social structure, reflecting specific social and professional attributes. Contrary to popular belief, ancient Indian texts such as the Vedas scarcely mention the term "Jaati"; instead, they elaborate on the Varna system. This Varna system, originating from sacred Hindu scriptures, aimed to organize society based on distinct roles and responsibilities.

At its core, the Varna system delineates four primary varnas: Brahmins, Kshatriyas, Vaishyas, and Shudras, each entrusted with specific duties. Brahmins, revered for their pursuit of knowledge and spirituality, occupied a preeminent position, followed by Kshatriyas responsible for governance and protection, Vaishyas engaged in commerce and agriculture, and Shudras fulfilling service-oriented roles.

Contrary to common misconceptions, varnas were not hereditary; rather, they were determined by an individual's chosen profession and aptitude. For instance, within a single family, individuals could belong to different varnas based on their talents and preferences. The system envisioned a societal structure devoid of hierarchy, wherein each varna held equal significance, akin to the interdependent parts of the human body.

Brahmins, analogous to the brain, encompassed scholars, teachers, and thinkers, guiding society with their wisdom. Kshatriyas, akin to protective hands, safeguarded societal interests, while Vaishyas, symbolizing the nurturing stomach, managed resources vital for sustenance. Shudras, akin to the hardworking legs, propelled society forward through their labor and dedication. This holistic perspective challenges modern misconceptions, unveiling a societal framework that valued every individual's contribution.

The significance of the Varna system lies in its endeavor to foster a harmonious societal structure, wherein individuals could contribute to collective well-being based on their inherent qualities and inclinations. Despite criticisms of its rigidity, understanding the origins of the Varna system offers profound insights into the historical, cultural, and religious contexts that underpinned ancient Hindu society.

However, over time, this system became corrupted, and the concept of varna became entrenched in birth, perpetuating a rigid social hierarchy that fostered division within Indian society. The once-flexible and merit-based Varna system gradually gave way to a system based solely on birth, resulting in a static and unyielding social order. Consequently, a blame game ensued, perpetuating societal discord. Regrettably, the consequences of this historical transformation continue to reverberate in modern times.

Now coming back to Brahmins, who also known as the priestly class, are an integral part of the Hindu society in India. They are considered to be the highest caste in the traditional Hindu caste system and are believed to have descended from the mouth of the Hindu god, Brahma. Brahmins are responsible for performing religious rituals, conducting ceremonies, and preserving the sacred texts of Hinduism.

However, despite their important role in

the society, Brahmins have often been portrayed in a negative light as oppressors and exploiters. This negative perception of Brahmins can be traced back to the colonial era when the British rulers used the caste system to divide and rule the Indian population. This led to the demonization of Brahmins as the privileged and dominant class, while the lower castes were portrayed as victims of their oppression.

In reality, Brahmins are not a homogenous group and their roles and status vary greatly depending on their region, occupation, and social background. While some Brahmins may have enjoyed certain privileges in the past, it is important to note that the caste system is not a static concept and has evolved over time. Today, many Brahmins are struggling with economic and social challenges, just like any other community.

Indeed, there existed a historical period where Brahmins occupied the apex of society, and regrettably, documentation reveals instances where a portion among them engaged in the practice of untouchability, often regarding themselves as superior. However, it would be unjust to categorize all Brahmins under the same umbrella and brand them as oppressors. The intricacies of the caste system demand a nuanced understanding, emphasizing the need to refrain from sweeping generalizations or stereotypes targeting any particular community. Just like any other social group, Brahmins possess a spectrum of attributes, encompassing strengths and weaknesses. It is imperative to transcend the constraints of negative stereotypes and instead recognize their manifold contributions to society.

Understanding the Brahmin community

The Brahmin community is one of the oldest and most influential communities in India. They are considered to be the highest caste in the Hindu social hierarchy and are known for their knowledge, wisdom, and spiritual practices. The word Brahmin is derived from the Sanskrit word "Brahman" which means the ultimate reality or the universal consciousness. The Brahmins are believed to be the descendants of the ancient Vedic sages and are considered to be the custodians of the Hindu religion and culture.

The Brahmin community is spread across different regions of India, with each region having its own distinct customs and traditions. However, there are certain common characteristics that are shared by all Brahmins, regardless of their geographical location. One of the most prominent features of the Brahmin community is their emphasis on education and learning. From a young age, Brahmin children are encouraged to pursue knowledge and are taught the scriptures and religious texts. This emphasis on education has resulted in a high literacy rate among the Brahmins, and many of them have excelled in various fields such as science, literature, and politics.

The Brahmins are also known for their strict adherence to the caste system as recorded in the modern history. They believe that they are born into their caste due to their good deeds in their past lives and that it is their duty to maintain their caste purity. This has led to the practice of endogamy, where marriage within the same caste is preferred but initially in the vedic times when Brahmins are created along with other 3 Varnas Kshatriyas, Vaishyas and Sudras it was not like that at that time Varna is decided by the action and quality and there was scope that by actions and quality a Brahmin can become a Shudra and similarly. The Brahmins also have a strict code of conduct and follow a set of rules and regulations prescribed by their scriptures. They are expected to lead a simple and austere life, free from materialistic desires.

The Brahmin community is deeply rooted in the Hindu religion and plays a crucial role in the preservation and propagation of Hinduism. They are the custodians of the Vedic knowledge and are responsible for performing religious rituals and ceremonies. The Brahmins are also the spiritual leaders of the community and are consulted for guidance and advice on matters of religion and spirituality. They are also responsible for teaching and passing on the religious traditions and customs to the younger generation.

Apart from their religious and spiritual roles, the Brahmins also hold significant positions in the society. In ancient times, they were the advisors and counselors to the kings and rulers. Even today, many Brahmins hold influential positions in the government, education, and other sectors. This has led to the perception that the Brahmins are a privileged community, which has often been a source of resentment and criticism from other castes.

However, it is important to note that the Brahmins are not a homogenous group and there is a lot of diversity within the community. There are different sub-castes and sects within the Brahmin community, each with its own set of customs and traditions. For example, the Smartha Brahmins follow the Advaita philosophy of Hinduism, while the Madhva Brahmins follow the Dvaita philosophy. Similarly, the Iyer Brahmins of South India have different customs and traditions compared to the Kashmiri Pandits of North India.

In recent times, the Brahmin community has faced criticism and backlash for their perceived dominance and privilege in the society. This has led to a growing awareness and debate within the community about the need for social reform and inclusivity. Many Brahmins have also taken up social causes and are actively involved in promoting education and social welfare in their communities.

The Brahmin community is a complex and diverse group with a rich cultural and religious heritage. They have played a significant role in shaping the Indian society and continue to be an influential community in the present times. While there are certain stereotypes and criticisms associated with the Brahmins, it is important to understand that they are not a monolithic group and have their own struggles and challenges. As India continues to evolve and progress, it is crucial to have a nuanced understanding of the Brahmin community and their contributions to the country.

The misconceptions and stereotypes surrounding Brahmins

The Brahmin community, deeply entrenched in the fabric of Indian society, has often been shrouded in a fog of misconceptions and stereotypes. These misinterpretations, fueled by a combination of historical distortions, cultural biases, and limited understanding, have contributed to a skewed perception of Brahmins and their role in society. To truly understand the Brahmin community and appreciate its contributions, it is imperative to unravel these misconceptions and shed light on the realities within.

One of the most prevalent misconceptions is the portrayal of Brahmins as an elitist and privileged class, detached from the struggles of everyday life. While it's undeniable that Brahmins historically held positions of influence due to their roles in education, religion, and governance, this portrayal oversimplifies the community's diversity. Brahmins hail from various socio-economic backgrounds, engaging in a myriad of occupations and pursuits. To paint them all with the same elitist brush is to ignore the nuanced realities within the community.

Another stereotype that plagues Brahmins is the perception of them as staunch traditionalists resistant to change and innovation. However, this overlooks the dynamic nature of Brahmin culture, which has continuously evolved and adapted over centuries. Brahmins have been pioneers in intellectual and cultural spheres, contributing significantly to fields such as philosophy, science, and literature. Their commitment to tradition does not preclude them from embracing progress and modernity.

Brahmins have unfairly been cast as the architects and enforcers of the caste system, perpetuating inequality and discrimination. While it's true that Brahmins historically held positions of authority within the caste hierarchy, attributing the entire system's existence solely to Brahmin influence oversimplifies a complex social phenomenon. Brahmins themselves have faced discrimination and marginalization based on caste, challenging the notion of Brahmins as the sole beneficiaries of the caste system.

Brahmins have been stereotyped as rigidly orthodox in their religious beliefs and practices. While they have played a significant role in preserving and propagating Hinduism, this stereotype overlooks the diversity of religious beliefs and practices within the Brahmin community. Brahmins exhibit a wide range of spiritual expressions, from orthodox to liberal interpretations. To homogenize

Brahmin religious identity is to disregard the rich tapestry of faith and belief within the community.

These misconceptions not only distort perceptions of Brahmins but also perpetuate social divisions and prejudices. It is crucial to recognize the humanity and diversity within the Brahmin community, acknowledging their contributions, challenges, and aspirations. By challenging these stereotypes and fostering dialogue and understanding, we can move towards a more inclusive society where individuals are not judged by preconceived notions but by the complexity of their character and actions.

The purpose of this book

At the core of every literary endeavor lies a driving purpose, a compelling reason that propels the author to embark on a journey of expression and discovery. The purpose of writing this book on Brahmins transcends mere academic inquiry; it is rooted in a profound commitment to fostering understanding, dispelling misconceptions, and celebrating the rich tapestry of Brahmin identity.

First and foremost, this book seeks to illuminate the complexities of Brahmin identity and the multifaceted role they have played in shaping Indian society. Through meticulous research and thoughtful analysis, it endeavors to unravel the layers of history, culture, and tradition that define the Brahmin community. By delving into their origins, duties, way of life, and contributions to various spheres of society, the book aims to provide readers with a comprehensive understanding of Brahmins beyond stereotypes and misconceptions.

Furthermore, the book aspires to challenge prevalent stereotypes and promote dialogue and empathy. By addressing misconceptions surrounding Brahmins and the caste system, it aims to foster a more nuanced and inclusive discourse on caste dynamics in India. Through empathetic storytelling and critical reflection, it endeavors to bridge divides and cultivate a deeper appreciation for the diversity and complexity of Indian society.

Moreover, this book serves as a call to action for social justice and equality. By shedding light on the challenges and inequalities faced by Brahmins, such as discrimination and stigma, it advocates for greater awareness and advocacy for marginalized communities within the Brahmin fold. Through highlighting issues such as reservation, inter-caste marriages, and cultural appropriation, it aims to spark conversations and inspire collective action towards a more equitable and just society.

Ultimately, the purpose of writing this book extends beyond the confines of academia; it is a testament to the power of storytelling and scholarship to effect positive change. By amplifying Brahmin voices, challenging stereotypes, and advocating for social justice, it seeks to contribute to a more inclusive and empathetic world where individuals are valued not for their social status or background, but for their humanity and contributions to society.

In essence, the purpose of this book is to inspire reflection, dialogue, and action—to provoke thought, challenge assumptions, and ultimately, to foster a more just and compassionate society for all.

Chapter 2: The Origins of Brahmins

Delving into the origins of Brahmins is akin to embarking on a journey through the annals of time, traversing the rich tapestry of Indian history, culture, and spirituality. At the heart of this exploration lies a profound inquiry into the genesis of a community that has left an indelible mark on the fabric of Indian society.

The origins of Brahmins can be traced back to the dawn of Indian civilization, rooted in the ancient scriptures known as the Vedas. These sacred texts, believed to be divinely revealed, serve as the foundational pillars of Hinduism and provide invaluable insights into the socio-religious landscape of ancient

India.

During the Vedic period, Brahmins emerged as a priestly class entrusted with the sacred task of preserving and transmitting Vedic knowledge. Their role was multifaceted, encompassing not only ritualistic duties but also intellectual pursuits such as recitation, interpretation, and commentary on the Vedas.

The term "Brahmin" itself is derived from the Sanskrit word "Brahmana," which signifies one who possesses knowledge of Brahman, the ultimate reality or cosmic consciousness in Hindu philosophy. Thus, Brahmins were regarded as custodians of spiritual wisdom, serving as intermediaries between the divine and the human realms.

Furthermore, Brahmins played a pivotal role in the social, cultural, and intellectual life of ancient India. They served as advisors to kings, educators to the masses, and custodians of ethical and moral values. Through their scholarly pursuits, Brahmins contributed to the development of various disciplines such as philosophy, linguistics, mathematics, astronomy, and medicine.

It is essential to acknowledge that the origins of Brahmins are not confined to a single historical moment or geographical location. Rather, they are intertwined with the complex tapestry of Indian society, influenced by diverse cultural, linguistic, and regional factors.

The evolution of Brahmin identity has been shaped by interactions with other social groups, migrations, invasions, and the spread of religious and philosophical movements. This dynamic process of cultural exchange and adaptation has contributed to the rich diversity within the Brahmin community, with distinct regional, linguistic, and sectarian variations.

Exploring the origins of Brahmins is an invitation to delve into the depths of Indian history and culture, unraveling the intricate threads that weave together the tapestry of Brahmin identity. It is a journey of discovery, reflection, and appreciation for the enduring legacy of a community that continues to shape the spiritual and intellectual landscape of India and beyond.

The Vedic period and the emergence of Brahmins

To understand the origins of Brahmins, one must journey back to the Vedic period, a pivotal epoch in Indian history that laid the foundation for Hinduism and shaped the cultural landscape of the subcontinent. The Vedic period witnessed the emergence of a complex socio-religious system characterized by the composition of the Vedas, sacred texts revered as the oldest scriptures of Hinduism.

At the heart of Vedic society were the Brahmins, a priestly class entrusted with the solemn duty of preserving and transmitting Vedic knowledge. The term "Brahmin" finds its roots in the Sanskrit word "Brahmana," signifying one who possesses knowledge of Brahman, the supreme cosmic spirit in

Hindu philosophy. Thus, Brahmins were revered as custodians of spiritual wisdom, serving as intermediaries between the divine and mortal realms.

The Rigveda, the oldest of the Vedas, provides valuable insights into the roles and responsibilities of Brahmins during the Vedic period. They were tasked with performing elaborate rituals, sacrifices, and ceremonies aimed at appeasing the gods and ensuring the cosmic order (Rta). These rituals, often accompanied by hymns and invocations, were meticulously performed to maintain harmony between the celestial and terrestrial realms.

Brahmins played a pivotal role in disseminating Vedic knowledge through oral tradition. They served as educators, transmitting sacred hymns, rituals, and philosophical insights to subsequent generations. This tradition of oral transmission ensured the preservation and continuity of Vedic teachings, laying the groundwork for the development of Hindu philosophical schools and religious practices.

Brahmins wielded considerable influence in the socio-political sphere of Vedic society. They served as advisors to kings and rulers, offering counsel on matters of governance, ethics, and morality. Their expertise in matters of ritual and cosmology endowed them with a position of authority and prestige, shaping the moral and ethical fabric of Vedic civilization.

However, it is essential to recognize that the emergence of Brahmins was not an isolated phenomenon but occurred within the broader context of Vedic society. The Vedic period witnessed the coexistence of various social groups, each with its own distinct roles and responsibilities. Brahmins, alongside Kshatriyas (warriors), Vaishyas (merchants and artisans), and Shudras (laborers), formed the four varnas, or social classes, delineated in Vedic texts.

The Vedic period and the emergence of Brahmins represent a pivotal chapter in Indian history, characterized by profound intellectual and spiritual inquiry. It was a time of cultural efflorescence, marked by the composition of sacred hymns, philosophical speculation, and ritual innovation. The legacy of Brahmins as custodians of Vedic wisdom continues to resonate in contemporary Hinduism, embodying the enduring spirit of spiritual inquiry and reverence for the divine.

In the vast expanse of ancient Indian civilization, the Brahmins occupied a pivotal position, their influence permeating every facet of societal existence. To comprehend the role of Brahmins in ancient society is to embark on a journey through the annals of history, exploring the multifaceted dimensions of their contributions and significance.

At the heart of Brahmin society lay the preservation and dissemination of sacred knowledge, particularly the Vedas—the foundational scriptures of Hinduism. Brahmins were revered as the custodians of this divine wisdom, entrusted with the solemn duty of performing rituals, reciting hymns, and interpreting the cosmic truths embedded within the sacred texts. Their expertise in Vedic rituals and ceremonies rendered them indispensable in mediating between the mortal realm and the divine, ensuring the cosmic order (dharma) was maintained.

Beyond their religious duties, Brahmins wielded considerable influence in matters of governance, serving as advisors to kings and rulers. Their erudition, wisdom, and ethical integrity made them invaluable counselors, guiding rulers in matters of statecraft, administration, and justice. The epics of ancient India, such as the Ramayana and Mahabharata, are replete with instances of Brahmin advisors playing pivotal roles in shaping political decisions and societal norms.

Furthermore, Brahmins occupied esteemed

positions as educators and scholars, disseminating knowledge and fostering intellectual inquiry. They established gurukuls (traditional schools) where pupils from diverse backgrounds received holistic education encompassing not only academic subjects but also moral and ethical teachings. Brahmin scholars made significant contributions to various fields of knowledge, including philosophy, astronomy, mathematics, linguistics, and medicine, laying the foundation for India's intellectual legacy.

In addition to their religious and scholarly pursuits, Brahmins also played a crucial role in upholding social order and moral values within ancient society. Their adherence to strict codes of conduct and ethical principles set the standard for righteous living, serving as exemplars of virtuous behavior for the broader community.

Brahmins were expected to embody qualities such as humility, compassion, and self-discipline, thereby guiding society towards spiritual upliftment and moral rectitude.

Moreover, Brahmins were patrons of art, literature, and culture, fostering creativity and aesthetic expression. They composed hymns, poems, and treatises on various subjects, enriching the cultural tapestry of ancient India. Their patronage of temples, festivals, and religious ceremonies contributed to the flourishing of artistic and architectural endeavors, leaving behind a rich legacy of cultural heritage that endures to this day.

In essence, the role of Brahmins in ancient society was multifaceted and far-reaching, encompassing religious, political, educational, and cultural spheres. Their influence extended beyond mere ritualistic duties, shaping the very fabric of Indian civilization and laying the groundwork for the spiritual and intellectual heritage that continues to resonate in contemporary times.

The importance of knowledge and education in Brahmin culture

In the intricate tapestry of Brahmin culture, the ethos of knowledge and education stands as a cornerstone, deeply embedded in the very fabric of their identity. This reverence for learning extends far beyond the acquisition of mere facts and figures; rather, it embodies a profound commitment to intellectual pursuit, spiritual enlightenment, and societal betterment.

Central to the importance of knowledge and education in Brahmin culture is the belief that true wisdom transcends the boundaries of worldly possessions and material wealth. Rooted in ancient scriptures such as the Vedas, Brahmins view knowledge as a sacred duty, a pathway to deeper understanding, and ultimately, to self-realization. The Rigveda, for instance, contains hymns composed by Brahmin sages that not only offer insights into cosmic principles but also serve as a testament to the intellectual prowess of ancient Brahmin scholars.

Beyond the realm of intellectual curiosity, Brahmin culture places a strong emphasis on the moral and ethical dimensions of education. Virtues such as humility, compassion, integrity, and self-discipline are not just ideals to be admired but qualities to be cultivated through rigorous study and introspection. The Mahabharata, an epic revered in Hinduism, provides numerous examples of Brahmin characters who embody these virtues, serving as moral compasses for society.

Furthermore, Brahmins uphold the tradition of knowledge transmission through the guru-shishya parampara, a sacred lineage of teacher-student relationships. This ancient tradition fosters a deep sense of reverence and intimacy between guru (teacher) and shishya (student), creating an environment conducive to learning and personal growth. Through this intimate mentorship, Brahmin students not only acquire knowledge but also imbibe the values and principles espoused by their teachers.

In the broader societal context, the importance of knowledge and education in Brahmin culture extends to the role

Brahmins play as educators, scholars, and advisors. Throughout history, Brahmins have served as custodians of knowledge, guiding society through periods of intellectual, cultural, and political transformation. From imparting Vedic wisdom to advising kings and rulers, Brahmins have played a pivotal role in shaping the intellectual and spiritual landscape of India.

Even in contemporary times, Brahmins continue to uphold the legacy of knowledge and education, adapting to modern educational systems while preserving traditional modes of learning. Many Brahmin scholars today actively engage in research, teaching, and intellectual discourse, contributing to advancements in various fields of study.

The importance of knowledge and education in Brahmin culture transcends mere academic pursuits; it embodies a holistic approach to intellectual, moral, and spiritual development. It is this dedication to learning and enlightenment that has enabled Brahmins to not only enrich their own lives but also to serve as beacons of wisdom and guidance for humanity.

Chapter 3: The Duties of a Brahmin

Within the intricate tapestry of Hindu society, the role of Brahmins stands as a beacon of guidance, wisdom, and spiritual enlightenment. Rooted deeply in ancient scriptures and cultural traditions, Brahmins are entrusted with sacred duties that transcend mere worldly obligations. This introduction seeks to illuminate the multifaceted responsibilities that define the duties of a Brahmin, shedding light on their role in maintaining social harmony, preserving knowledge, and fostering spiritual growth.

At the heart of Brahmin duties lie four fundamental pillars: studying, teaching, performing rituals, and giving charity. These duties, outlined in ancient texts such as the Manusmriti and the Vedas, serve as guiding principles for Brahmin conduct and societal engagement. Through rigorous study and intellectual inquiry, Brahmins acquire sacred knowledge and wisdom, which they then impart to others through teaching and dissemination. Additionally, Brahmins are tasked with performing rituals and ceremonies that uphold religious traditions and foster spiritual well-being within the community. Lastly, the duty of charity underscores the Brahmin's commitment to social welfare and compassion towards others.

As we delve deeper into the intricacies of Brahmin duties, we uncover a tapestry of tradition, ethics, and spiritual devotion that continues to shape the cultural landscape of Hindu society. Through this exploration, we aim to gain a deeper understanding of the profound responsibilities entrusted to Brahmins and the enduring legacy of their contributions to society.

The four main duties of a Brahmin: studying, teaching, performing rituals, and giving charity

Embedded within the intricate fabric of Brahmin culture are four fundamental duties that serve as guiding principles for their conduct and societal engagement. These duties, rooted in ancient scriptures and upheld through generations, embody the essence of Brahmin identity and the responsibilities entrusted to them within Hindu society. Let us embark on a comprehensive exploration of each of these duties: studying, teaching, performing rituals, and giving charity.

Studying:

At the core of Brahmin identity lies a deep reverence for knowledge and intellectual inquiry. The duty of studying encompasses not only the acquisition of worldly knowledge but also the pursuit of spiritual wisdom and enlightenment. From a young age, Brahmin children are encouraged to immerse themselves in the study of sacred texts such as the Vedas, Upanishads, and other scriptures. This rigorous pursuit of knowledge extends throughout their lives, as Brahmins engage in lifelong learning and intellectual exploration. Through the study of scriptures, philosophy, mathematics, astronomy, and other disciplines, Brahmins seek to deepen their understanding of the cosmos, the self, and the divine.

Teaching:

The duty of teaching is intricately intertwined with the duty of studying, as Brahmins are not only seekers of knowledge but also its custodians and disseminators. Guided by the principle of guru-shishya parampara, or teacher-student tradition, Brahmins pass down their wisdom and learning to future generations. Through formal education, informal mentoring, and spiritual guidance, Brahmin teachers play a pivotal role in shaping the intellectual and moral development of their students. Whether in traditional gurukulas (schools) or modern educational institutions, Brahmin educators strive to inspire a love for learning and instill values of integrity, compassion, and service.

Performing Rituals:

Central to Brahmin identity is the

performance of rituals and ceremonies that uphold religious traditions and foster spiritual well-being within the community. Brahmins are trained in the intricate rituals outlined in sacred texts such as the Vedas and the Smritis, which govern every aspect of religious life, from birth to death. Whether it be the performance of daily prayers (sandhyavandanam), rites of passage ceremonies (samskaras), or elaborate Vedic sacrifices (yajnas), Brahmins serve as conduits between the divine and the human realms. Through their meticulous adherence to ritual purity and devotion, Brahmins ensure the continuity of religious traditions and the preservation of sacred knowledge.

Giving Charity:

The duty of giving charity, or dana, is deeply ingrained in Brahmin culture as an expression of compassion, generosity, and social responsibility. Brahmins are enjoined to share their knowledge, wealth, and resources with those in need, thereby alleviating suffering and promoting social welfare. Whether through acts of philanthropy, supporting educational initiatives, or providing spiritual guidance, Brahmins contribute to the well-being of society and uphold the principles of dharma (righteousness) and seva (selfless service). By embodying the spirit of charity, Brahmins seek to foster harmony and inclusivity within their communities and society at large.

The four main duties of a Brahmin—studying, teaching, performing rituals, and giving charity—represent a holistic approach to life guided by the pursuit of knowledge, spiritual growth, and service to humanity. It is through the fulfillment of these duties that Brahmins uphold the timeless values of their culture and contribute to the greater good of society.

The significance of each duty in maintaining balance in society

Within the framework of Brahmin culture, each duty—studying, teaching, performing rituals, and giving charity—plays a crucial role in upholding the delicate balance within society. These duties are not merely individual obligations but integral components of a larger societal ecosystem, contributing to the harmonious functioning of communities and the preservation of moral, ethical, and spiritual values.

Studying:

The duty of studying holds immense significance in maintaining balance within society by nurturing intellectual curiosity, fostering critical thinking, and preserving cultural heritage. Through rigorous study of sacred texts and philosophical inquiry, Brahmins cultivate a deep understanding of dharma (righteousness), karma (action), and moksha (liberation), which form the moral and spiritual foundation of Hindu society. This pursuit of knowledge not only enriches individual lives but also contributes to the collective wisdom of communities, guiding them towards ethical conduct and spiritual fulfillment.

The duty of studying holds immense significance in maintaining balance within society by nurturing intellectual curiosity, fostering critical thinking, and preserving cultural heritage. For example, during the Vedic period, Brahmin scholars meticulously studied and memorized the sacred texts known as the Vedas, preserving ancient wisdom and spiritual knowledge for future generations. Their dedication to scholarship laid the foundation for the intellectual and spiritual development of Hindu society, fostering a deep understanding of ethical principles, cosmic order, and the nature of existence.

Teaching:

The duty of teaching complements the duty of studying by ensuring the transmission of knowledge and values from one generation to the next. Through their role as educators and mentors, Brahmins play a vital role in shaping the moral character, intellectual development, and cultural identity of society. By imparting moral and ethical teachings, instilling a sense of social responsibility, and fostering empathy and compassion, Brahmin teachers contribute to the holistic development of individuals and the cultivation of a harmonious and virtuous society.

The duty of teaching complements the duty of studying by ensuring the transmission of knowledge and values from one generation to the next. Throughout history, Brahmin teachers have played pivotal roles in shaping the moral character, intellectual development, and cultural identity of society. One notable example is the ancient system of gurukulas, where Brahmin students lived with their teachers in a residential setting, imbibing not only academic knowledge but also moral and ethical teachings through personal mentorship. The teachings of revered gurus such as Adi Shankaracharya, who established monastic orders and propagated Advaita Vedanta philosophy, continue to inspire spiritual seekers and scholars to this day.

Performing Rituals:

Central to Brahmin culture is the duty of performing rituals and ceremonies, which serve as spiritual anchors and communal expressions of faith and devotion. These rituals, rooted in ancient scriptures and guided by tradition, play a pivotal role in reinforcing social cohesion, fostering a sense of belonging, and maintaining spiritual equilibrium within society. Through their meticulous observance of rituals, Brahmins uphold the sanctity of religious traditions, preserve cultural heritage, and facilitate communal bonding, thereby fostering a sense of unity and harmony among diverse social groups.

Central to Brahmin culture is the duty of performing rituals and ceremonies, which serve as spiritual anchors and communal expressions of faith and devotion. Historical examples abound of Brahmins meticulously performing rituals to uphold religious traditions and foster spiritual well-being within society. For instance, during the Gupta period in ancient India, Brahmin priests conducted elaborate Vedic sacrifices (yajnas) to invoke divine blessings and ensure prosperity for the kingdom. These rituals not only strengthened the bond between rulers and subjects but also reinforced social cohesion and collective identity through shared religious practices.

Giving Charity:

The duty of giving charity embodies the spirit of compassion, generosity, and social responsibility, serving as a powerful mechanism for promoting equity, alleviating suffering, and fostering inclusivity within society. By sharing their knowledge, wealth, and resources with those in need, Brahmins mitigate disparities, promote social welfare, and cultivate a culture of empathy and solidarity. Through acts of charity such as feeding the hungry, providing educational opportunities, and supporting marginalized communities, Brahmins contribute to the creation of a more just, compassionate, and egalitarian society.

The duty of giving charity embodies the spirit of compassion, generosity, and social responsibility, serving as a powerful mechanism for promoting equity, alleviating suffering, and fostering inclusivity within society. Throughout history, Brahmins have been renowned for their philanthropy and support of social welfare initiatives. For example, during the Maurya and Gupta empires, wealthy Brahmin families funded the construction of hospitals, schools, and public infrastructure, providing essential services to the less fortunate and contributing to the overall well-being of society. Additionally, Brahmin scholars often donated land and resources to support educational institutions and libraries, ensuring access to knowledge and learning for future generations.

The significance of each duty in maintaining balance in society lies in their collective impact on the moral, ethical, and spiritual fabric of communities. By fulfilling their respective duties with diligence, integrity, and compassion, Brahmins uphold the timeless values of their culture and contribute to the creation of a harmonious and virtuous society characterized by mutual respect, social cohesion, and spiritual flourishing.

How these duties have evolved over time

The duties of a Brahmin, rooted in ancient scriptures and cultural traditions, have undergone a profound evolution over the course of history. From the Vedic period to the present day, these duties have adapted to changing societal dynamics, technological advancements, and philosophical shifts, while retaining their core principles of knowledge, service, and spiritual devotion. Let us delve into a detailed exploration of how these duties have evolved over time:

Studying:

In ancient times, the duty of studying was primarily centered around the memorization and recitation of sacred texts such as the Vedas, Upanishads, and Smritis. Brahmin students underwent rigorous training in gurukulas (traditional schools) under the guidance of learned gurus, where they immersed themselves in the study of scripture, philosophy, and other disciplines. Over time, with the advent of written texts and the proliferation of educational institutions, the methods of study diversified, encompassing a broader range of subjects and pedagogical approaches. Today, Brahmins continue to uphold the tradition of studying through formal education, self-directed learning, and engagement with contemporary scholarship, adapting to the demands of a rapidly changing world while remaining grounded in the timeless wisdom of their cultural heritage.

Teaching:

The duty of teaching has evolved alongside changes in educational practices, social structures, and technological advancements. In ancient times, Brahmin teachers played a central role in transmitting knowledge and values through oral tradition and direct mentorship. As society progressed, formal educational institutions such as universities, schools, and colleges emerged, providing new avenues for teaching and learning. Brahmins continued to occupy prominent roles as educators, scholars, and mentors, adapting their teaching methods to suit the needs of diverse student populations and evolving pedagogical trends. Today, Brahmins continue to uphold the tradition of teaching through various platforms such as schools, universities, online courses, and community workshops, leveraging modern technologies to reach a wider audience and disseminate knowledge.

Performing Rituals:

The duty of performing rituals has evolved in response to changes in religious practices, societal norms, and cultural values. In ancient times, Brahmins served as custodians of religious rituals and ceremonies, conducting elaborate sacrifices, rites of passage, and worship ceremonies as prescribed in sacred texts. With the passage of time, the emphasis on ritual purity and adherence to tradition gradually gave way to more inclusive and flexible approaches to religious worship. Brahmins adapted their rituals to accommodate changing social dynamics, emerging philosophical schools, and the influence of foreign traditions. Today, while traditional rituals continue to be practiced, Brahmins also engage in innovative forms of worship, community service, and spiritual outreach, catering to the diverse needs and preferences of modern society.

Giving Charity:

The duty of giving charity has evolved in response to shifts in economic systems, social structures, and cultural values. In ancient times, charity was primarily practiced through acts of hospitality, almsgiving, and patronage of religious institutions. Brahmins supported the needy, funded educational initiatives, and contributed to the upkeep of temples, ashrams, and other charitable institutions. Over time, as society became more complex and interconnected, the concept of charity expanded to include philanthropy, social activism, and advocacy for social justice. Brahmins played key roles in reform movements, humanitarian causes, and community development projects, leveraging their resources, influence, and expertise to address pressing societal issues. Today, Brahmins continue to uphold the tradition of giving charity through various means such as donations, volunteerism, and advocacy, contributing to the well-being of society and the advancement of human welfare.

The evolution of Brahmin duties over time reflects a dynamic interplay between tradition and innovation, continuity and change. While the core principles of knowledge, service, and spiritual devotion remain constant, the methods and practices through which these duties are fulfilled have evolved in response to the ever-changing demands and challenges of the world. Through adaptation, resilience, and a commitment to their cultural heritage, Brahmins continue to uphold their duties and contribute to the flourishing of society in myriad ways.

Chapter 4: The Brahmin Way of Life

Steeped in tradition, guided by principles, and anchored in spiritual devotion, the Brahmin way of life encapsulates a profound philosophy that has endured through centuries. Rooted in the ancient scriptures and cultural practices of Hinduism, the Brahmin way of life encompasses a holistic approach to existence, emphasizing values such as simplicity, non-violence, and self-discipline.

At its core, the Brahmin way of life is characterized by a deep reverence for knowledge, spiritual growth, and ethical conduct. Brahmins, as custodians of sacred wisdom and guardians of tradition, strive to embody the ideals of righteousness (dharma), duty (karma), and liberation (moksha). Through rigorous study, contemplation, and adherence to religious rituals, Brahmins seek to cultivate inner peace, moral integrity, and spiritual enlightenment.

Moreover, the Brahmin way of life places a strong emphasis on selflessness, service to others, and humility. Brahmins are encouraged to lead lives of simplicity and moderation, eschewing materialism and worldly attachments in favor of spiritual pursuits and selfless acts of charity. By embodying these principles in their daily lives, Brahmins aspire to uplift themselves and contribute positively to the well-being of society.

Brahmin way of life, uncovering its timeless

wisdom, enduring values, and profound insights into the human condition. Through this exploration, we aim to gain a deeper understanding of the principles that shape Brahmin identity and the significance of their way of life in the broader context of Hindu culture and spirituality.

The principles and values that guide Brahmin lifestyle

At the heart of Brahmin lifestyle lies a rich tapestry of principles and values that have been passed down through generations, shaping the cultural identity and spiritual ethos of this esteemed community. Rooted in ancient scriptures, philosophical traditions, and cultural practices, these guiding principles offer a roadmap for ethical conduct, spiritual growth, and societal harmony. Let us embark on a comprehensive exploration of the principles and values that form the bedrock of Brahmin lifestyle:

1. Pursuit of Knowledge (Jnana):

Central to Brahmin lifestyle is an unwavering commitment to the pursuit of knowledge in all its forms—spiritual, philosophical, and intellectual. Brahmins are enjoined to engage in rigorous study, contemplation, and dialogue, seeking to unravel the mysteries of the cosmos and the nature of the self. This quest for knowledge is not merely an academic pursuit but a sacred duty, a pathway to spiritual enlightenment, and a means of serving humanity.

Central to Brahmin lifestyle is an unwavering commitment to the pursuit of knowledge in all its forms—spiritual, philosophical, and intellectual. For instance, ancient Brahmin scholars like Adi Shankaracharya dedicated their lives to the study and interpretation of scriptures, expounding profound philosophical doctrines that continue to inspire seekers of truth. Similarly, modern Brahmin intellectuals engage in scientific research, philosophical inquiry, and academic pursuits, contributing to advancements in various fields of study.

2. Spiritual Devotion (Bhakti):

Brahmin lifestyle is infused with a deep sense of spiritual devotion and reverence for the divine. Through prayer, meditation, and ritual worship, Brahmins seek to cultivate a personal relationship with the divine and experience a profound sense of connection and unity with the cosmos. This devotion is expressed through acts of piety, humility, and surrender, as Brahmins surrender their ego and desires to the divine will.

Brahmin lifestyle is infused with a deep sense of spiritual devotion and reverence for the divine. For example, Brahmin priests perform elaborate rituals and ceremonies in temples, invoking the blessings of the gods and goddesses for the well-being of the community. Devotional practices such as chanting of mantras, singing of hymns, and recitation of scriptures are integral aspects of Brahmin spiritual life, fostering a sense of connection and devotion to the divine.

3. Moral Integrity (Dharma):

Integral to Brahmin lifestyle is a steadfast adherence to moral and ethical principles, encapsulated in the concept of dharma. Brahmins are expected to uphold righteousness, honesty, and integrity in all aspects of life, fulfilling their duties and responsibilities with sincerity and humility. Dharma serves as a moral compass, guiding Brahmins in their interactions with others and their engagement with the world.

Integral to Brahmin lifestyle is a steadfast adherence to moral and ethical principles, encapsulated in the concept of dharma. Brahmins are expected to uphold righteousness, honesty, and integrity in all aspects of life. For instance, ancient Brahmin kings such as Raja Harishchandra were renowned for their adherence to dharma, ruling with justice and compassion, even in the face of adversity. Similarly, modern Brahmins strive to live by ethical principles, upholding honesty, integrity, and social responsibility in their personal and professional lives.

4. Non-Violence (Ahimsa):

Ahimsa, or non-violence, is a foundational principle that underpins Brahmin lifestyle. Brahmins are called to practice compassion, kindness, and non-violence towards all living beings, recognizing the interconnectedness and sacredness of life. This principle extends not only to physical actions but also to thoughts, words, and intentions, fostering harmony and respect for all sentient beings.

Ahimsa, or non-violence, is a foundational principle that underpins Brahmin lifestyle. For example, Mahatma Gandhi, a prominent Brahmin leader, championed the principle of ahimsa as a means of social and political change, leading India to independence through non-violent resistance. Similarly, Brahmin communities advocate for animal welfare, environmental conservation, and peace-building initiatives, embodying the spirit of non-violence in their actions and advocacy efforts.

5. Self-Discipline (Tapas):

Brahmin lifestyle emphasizes the importance of self-discipline and austerity as a means of purifying the mind, body, and spirit. Through practices such as fasting, meditation, and self-restraint, Brahmins seek to overcome worldly desires, cultivate inner strength, and attain spiritual liberation. Tapas is seen as a transformative process that leads to self-mastery and spiritual growth.

Brahmin lifestyle emphasizes the

importance of self-discipline and austerity as a means of purifying the mind, body, and spirit. For instance, ancient Brahmin sages undertook rigorous penances and ascetic practices to attain spiritual realization. Today, Brahmins continue to practice self-discipline through rituals such as fasting, meditation, and self-restraint, cultivating inner strength and resilience in the face of life's challenges.

6. Service to Humanity (Seva):

An integral aspect of Brahmin lifestyle is the ethos of selfless service to humanity. Brahmins are called to use their knowledge, skills, and resources for the betterment of society, serving as guides, mentors, and benefactors to those in need. This spirit of seva embodies the principle of universal brotherhood and underscores the interconnectedness of all beings.

An integral aspect of Brahmin lifestyle is the ethos of selfless service to humanity. For example, Brahmin communities organize philanthropic initiatives such as food drives, healthcare camps, and educational programs to uplift marginalized communities and alleviate suffering. Similarly, Brahmin individuals volunteer their time and expertise in various social and humanitarian causes, embodying the principle of seva and making a positive impact in the lives of others.

The principles and values that guide Brahmin lifestyle reflect a holistic approach to life that integrates spiritual, moral, and ethical dimensions. Through their adherence to these principles, Brahmins aspire to lead lives of wisdom, integrity, and compassion, contributing to the well-being of society and the upliftment of humanity as a whole.

Within the intricate tapestry of Brahmin lifestyle, the principles of simplicity, non-violence, and self-control stand as pillars, guiding individuals towards a life of moral integrity, spiritual growth, and societal harmony. Rooted in ancient scriptures, philosophical traditions, and cultural practices, these values shape the ethical conduct and character of Brahmins, reflecting a profound commitment to living in harmony with oneself, others, and the world at large. Let us delve into a detailed exploration of the emphasis on simplicity, non-violence, and self-control within Brahmin lifestyle:

1. Simplicity (Sauca):

Simplicity lies at the core of Brahmin lifestyle, advocating for a life of moderation, frugality, and contentment. Brahmins are encouraged to embrace a minimalist approach to material possessions, eschewing excessive wealth, luxury, and extravagance in favor of a simpler way of life. This emphasis on simplicity fosters a sense of detachment from worldly attachments, allowing Brahmins to focus their energies on spiritual pursuits and inner fulfillment. For example, ancient Brahmin ascetics renounced worldly comforts and lived austere lives in forests or monastic communities, devoting themselves to meditation, contemplation, and self-realization.

Simplicity lies at the core of Brahmin lifestyle, advocating for a life of moderation, frugality, and contentment. For example, ancient Brahmin ascetics, such as those belonging to the Sramana tradition, renounced material possessions and lived minimalist lives focused on spiritual pursuits. One such notable figure is Sage Gautama Buddha, who, before attaining enlightenment, famously renounced his princely life and lived as an ascetic, practicing austerity and simplicity in pursuit of spiritual realization.

2. Non-Violence (Ahimsa):

Non-violence occupies a central place in Brahmin lifestyle, reflecting a deep reverence for life and a commitment to compassion, kindness, and harmlessness towards all living beings. Brahmins adhere to the principle of ahimsa not only in their actions but also in their thoughts, words, and intentions, recognizing the interconnectedness and sanctity of all life forms. This emphasis on non-violence extends beyond physical harm to encompass emotional, psychological, and spiritual well-being, fostering a culture of empathy, respect, and non-aggression. For instance, Brahmin communities advocate for vegetarianism, animal welfare, and peace-building initiatives, embodying the spirit of ahimsa in their daily lives and societal engagements.

Non-violence occupies a central place in Brahmin lifestyle, reflecting a deep reverence for life and a commitment to compassion, kindness, and harmlessness towards all living beings. Historical figures like Mahavira, a contemporary of Gautama Buddha and the founder of Jainism, exemplified the principle of ahimsa through his teachings and lifestyle. Mahavira preached non-violence not only towards humans but also towards animals and advocated for vegetarianism as a means of practicing ahimsa.

3. Self-Control (Dama):

Self-control is regarded as a foundational virtue within Brahmin lifestyle, enabling individuals to govern their desires, impulses, and emotions with equanimity and restraint. Brahmins cultivate inner discipline through practices such as meditation, mindfulness, and self-awareness, seeking to transcend the fluctuations of the mind and attain spiritual liberation. This emphasis on self-control empowers Brahmins to overcome negative tendencies such as greed, anger, and attachment, fostering inner peace, clarity, and resilience in the face of life's challenges. For example, Brahmin practitioners of yoga and meditation engage in rigorous training to cultivate mastery over the mind and senses, harnessing their inner strength to navigate the complexities of existence with grace and wisdom.

Self-control is regarded as a foundational virtue within Brahmin lifestyle, enabling individuals to govern their desires, impulses, and emotions with equanimity and restraint. A historical example of self-control can be found in the life of Swami Vivekananda, a prominent Brahmin philosopher and spiritual leader. Vivekananda practiced rigorous discipline and self-control throughout his life, as evidenced by his austere lifestyle, dedicated meditation practices, and unwavering commitment to his mission of spreading Vedanta philosophy and spiritual wisdom.

The emphasis on simplicity, non-violence, and self-control within Brahmin lifestyle reflects a profound commitment to ethical conduct, spiritual growth, and societal harmony. Through their adherence to these values, Brahmins aspire to cultivate lives of integrity, compassion, and inner fulfillment, serving as beacons of light and inspiration in a world often overshadowed by materialism, aggression, and discord.

The importance of spiritual and moral development in Brahmin culture

Spiritual and moral development forms the cornerstone of Brahmin culture, shaping the identity, values, and worldview of this esteemed community. Rooted in ancient scriptures, philosophical teachings, and cultural practices, the emphasis on spiritual and moral growth reflects a profound commitment to inner transformation, ethical conduct, and the pursuit of higher truths. Let us delve into a detailed exploration of the importance of spiritual and moral development in Brahmin culture:

1. Connection to Divine Essence:

Brahmin culture places great importance on cultivating a deep connection with the divine essence that pervades all existence. Through rituals, prayers, and meditation practices, Brahmins seek to transcend the limitations of the material world and commune with the divine presence within themselves and the cosmos. This spiritual quest serves as a guiding light, illuminating the path towards self-realization, enlightenment, and union with the ultimate reality.

2. Ethical Foundation:

Moral development forms an integral aspect of Brahmin culture, providing a solid ethical foundation for individual conduct and societal interactions. Brahmins are guided by the principles of dharma (righteousness), which dictate virtuous behavior, honesty, integrity, and compassion towards all beings. Moral development involves the cultivation of noble qualities such as truthfulness, generosity, humility, and forgiveness, fostering a culture of ethical conduct and social responsibility within Brahmin communities.

3. Inner Transformation:

Spiritual and moral development in Brahmin culture is not merely an external adherence to religious rituals or ethical norms but a profound process of inner transformation. Brahmins engage in practices such as self-reflection, self-discipline, and self-inquiry to purify the mind, cultivate virtues, and overcome negative tendencies. This inner journey leads to a deepening of self-awareness, emotional maturity, and spiritual growth, enabling Brahmins to transcend egoic limitations and realize their true nature as divine beings.

4. Role in Society:

The importance of spiritual and moral development extends beyond individual growth to the broader societal context. Brahmins, as spiritual leaders, educators, and moral guides, play a pivotal role in nurturing the spiritual and moral fabric of society. Through their teachings, exemplary conduct, and compassionate service, Brahmins inspire others to lead lives of integrity, righteousness, and service to humanity, thereby contributing to the upliftment and welfare of society as a whole.

5. Preservation of Cultural Heritage:

Spiritual and moral development in Brahmin culture is intricately linked to the preservation and transmission of cultural heritage and sacred wisdom. Brahmins serve as custodians of ancient scriptures, philosophical teachings, and cultural practices, passing down this rich legacy from generation to generation. By embodying the timeless values of spiritual wisdom, moral integrity, and ethical conduct, Brahmins ensure the continuity and vitality of their cultural heritage for future generations.

6. Compassionate Service:

Brahmin culture emphasizes the importance of compassionate service (seva) as a means of expressing spiritual devotion and fulfilling one's moral duty. Brahmins engage in various forms of charitable activities, including providing food, shelter, education, and healthcare to those in need. This selfless service not only alleviates the suffering of others but also cultivates empathy, kindness, and humility within the individual, fostering a deeper connection to humanity and the divine.

7. Pursuit of Self-Realization:

Central to Brahmin culture is the pursuit of self-realization (atma-jnana), the direct experience of one's true nature as the divine Self. Brahmins engage in spiritual practices such as meditation, contemplation, and self-inquiry to transcend the limitations of the ego and realize their innate divinity. This quest for self-realization leads to profound inner peace, fulfillment, and liberation from the cycle of birth and death, enabling Brahmins to live in harmony with the cosmic order (dharma).

8. Role Models and Leadership:

Brahmin culture places a strong emphasis on cultivating exemplary character and leadership qualities as a means of inspiring others and guiding society towards higher ideals. Brahmin leaders, whether spiritual teachers, scholars, or social activists, serve as role models of moral integrity, wisdom, and compassion, inspiring others to emulate their virtues and contribute positively to the welfare of society. By embodying these ideals, Brahmins fulfill their sacred duty (swadharma) to lead by example and uplift humanity.

9. Integration of Spiritual and Mundane Life:

Brahmin culture advocates for the integration of spiritual values into all aspects of life, including family, work, and social relationships. Brahmins strive to maintain a balance between their spiritual pursuits and worldly responsibilities, recognizing that spiritual growth can be cultivated in everyday activities. By infusing their daily lives with mindfulness, gratitude, and devotion, Brahmins bridge the gap between the sacred and the mundane, leading lives imbued with spiritual meaning and purpose.

10. Contribution to Universal Harmony:

Ultimately, the importance of spiritual and moral development in Brahmin culture extends beyond individual and societal boundaries to encompass the creation of universal harmony and global peace. Brahmins aspire to cultivate virtues such as love, compassion, and forgiveness that transcend cultural, religious, and ideological differences, fostering a sense of unity and interconnectedness among all beings. Through their commitment to spiritual and moral values, Brahmins strive to create a world where peace, justice, and harmony prevail, fulfilling the ancient Vedic vision of Vasudhaiva Kutumbakam (the world is one family).

The importance of spiritual and moral development in Brahmin culture lies in its profound implications for individual growth, societal harmony, and cultural preservation. By nurturing spiritual awareness, moral integrity, and ethical conduct, Brahmins aspire to embody the highest ideals of human potential and contribute to the creation of a more enlightened, compassionate, and harmonious world.

Chapter 5: The Brahmin and Caste System

The intricacies of the caste system in India have long fascinated scholars and observers, with Brahmins occupying a central position within this social hierarchy. The relationship between Brahmins and the caste system is complex, marked by historical evolution, cultural practices, and contemporary interpretations. In this exploration, we embark on a journey to unravel the nuances of the Brahmin caste identity and its interactions with the broader caste system.

At the heart of understanding the Brahmin

and caste system lies a recognition of historical contexts and cultural dynamics. The caste system, originating from ancient Vedic scriptures, initially conceptualized society as a varna (type) system, organizing individuals into four primary varnas based on their occupational roles. Brahmins, as the priestly class entrusted with spiritual knowledge and rituals, occupied the highest varna, reflecting the societal reverence for wisdom and learning.

However, over time, the varna system evolved into a rigid social hierarchy, with birth determining one's caste and opportunities. This transformation led to the entrenchment of caste-based discrimination, marginalization of certain groups, and perpetuation of social inequalities. Within this framework, Brahmins came to be associated not only with spiritual authority but also with privilege and power, exacerbating tensions and disparities within society.

Yet, it is essential to acknowledge the diverse realities and perspectives within the Brahmin community regarding the caste system. While some Brahmins have benefited from caste-based privileges, others have challenged caste discrimination and advocated for social justice. Additionally, the caste system itself is not monolithic, exhibiting variations across regions, communities, and historical periods.

In this exploration, we delve into the complexities, contradictions, and lived experiences surrounding the Brahmin and caste system, aiming to foster a nuanced understanding that goes beyond stereotypes and oversimplifications.

Through this journey, we seek to shed light on the multifaceted nature of caste dynamics in India and the role of Brahmins within this intricate social tapestry.

The role of Brahmins in the caste system

The caste system in India is a complex social structure that has shaped the dynamics of society for millennia, with Brahmins occupying a significant position within this framework. The role of Brahmins in the caste system is multifaceted, influenced by historical, cultural, and religious factors that have evolved over time. Let us delve into a detailed exploration of the role of Brahmins in the caste system:

1. Spiritual Authority and Ritual Purity:

Historically, Brahmins have been assigned the role of priests and custodians of spiritual knowledge in Hindu society. As the highest varna in the caste hierarchy, Brahmins were entrusted with performing religious rituals, interpreting sacred scriptures, and imparting spiritual teachings to the community. Their association with purity and sanctity lent them significant influence and authority in matters of religious practice and social conduct.

Historically, Brahmins held significant influence as custodians of spiritual knowledge and ritual expertise. One prominent example is Adi Shankaracharya, a revered Brahmin philosopher and theologian who revitalized Hinduism through his teachings and establishment of monastic orders. Shankaracharya's philosophical works and spiritual leadership continue to inspire millions of followers to this day, highlighting the enduring influence of Brahmins in matters of spirituality and religious practice.

2. Social Status and Privilege:

Brahmins traditionally enjoyed a position of privilege and prestige within the caste system, owing to their role as custodians of knowledge and culture. They often held positions of power and influence in society, serving as advisors to kings, educators to the elite, and arbiters of moral conduct. This elevated status granted Brahmins access to resources, opportunities, and social networks that reinforced their position at the apex of the social hierarchy.

During the ancient and medieval periods, Brahmins enjoyed privileged positions in society, often serving as advisors to kings and rulers. An illustrative example is Chanakya, also known as Kautilya or Vishnugupta, a Brahmin scholar and statesman who played a pivotal role in the establishment of the Maurya Empire. Chanakya's political acumen and strategic insights contributed to the rise of Chandragupta Maurya as a powerful emperor, showcasing the socio-political influence wielded by Brahmins in shaping dynastic politics and governance.

3. Cultural Gatekeeping and Social Norms:

Brahmins played a crucial role in upholding and perpetuating caste-based social norms and practices. Through their religious authority and cultural influence, Brahmins reinforced caste distinctions, prescribed codes of conduct, and sanctioned social hierarchies. They determined rituals, customs, and traditions that delineated social boundaries and regulated interactions between different caste groups.

Brahmins played a central role in upholding caste-based social norms and customs through their religious authority. For instance, the Manusmriti, an ancient legal text attributed to the sage Manu, codified caste-based regulations and delineated social roles and responsibilities. Brahmin scholars were instrumental in interpreting and enforcing these norms, thereby reinforcing caste distinctions and societal hierarchies.

4. Education and Intellectual Leadership:

Education has historically been a hallmark of Brahmin culture, with Brahmins being the primary educators and scholars in ancient India. Brahmin intellectuals contributed significantly to the preservation and dissemination of knowledge in fields such as philosophy, literature, science, and astrology. Their dominance in educational institutions and intellectual circles reinforced their status as the intellectual elite of society.

Throughout history, Brahmins have been at the forefront of intellectual pursuits and educational institutions. An exemplary figure is Aryabhata, an ancient Brahmin mathematician and astronomer who made significant contributions to the fields of mathematics and astronomy. Aryabhata's groundbreaking work, including his treatise Aryabhatiya, advanced scientific knowledge and laid the foundation for future discoveries, highlighting the intellectual leadership of Brahmins in ancient India.

5. Evolution and Adaptation:

While Brahmins have traditionally occupied privileged positions within the caste system, their role has evolved and adapted to changing socio-economic and political landscapes. With the advent of colonialism, urbanization, and modernization, Brahmins faced challenges to their traditional authority and influence. Yet, many Brahmins have also been at the forefront of social reform movements, advocating for caste equality, social justice, and inclusive development.

In the modern era, Brahmins have adapted to changing social, economic, and political contexts while retaining their cultural heritage. Swami Vivekananda, a Brahmin monk and spiritual leader, exemplifies this adaptation through his efforts to revitalize Hinduism and promote Vedanta philosophy in the late 19th century. Vivekananda's message of universal brotherhood and spiritual empowerment resonated with people across the globe, demonstrating the continued relevance and adaptability of Brahmin ideals in contemporary society.

6. Legal and Judicial Authority:

In addition to their religious and cultural roles, Brahmins historically held positions of authority in legal and judicial matters. They served as judges, legal advisors, and arbitrators, applying principles of dharma (righteousness) to resolve disputes and administer justice within their communities. Brahmin jurists played a crucial role in interpreting and codifying customary laws and legal codes, shaping the legal framework of traditional Indian society.

Brahmins held positions of authority in legal and judicial matters, contributing to the development of legal systems in ancient India. One notable example is Yajnavalkya, an ancient sage and jurist who authored the Yajnavalkya Smriti, a legal text that served as a foundational source of Hindu law. Yajnavalkya's jurisprudence provided guidance on matters of family law, property rights, and inheritance, shaping legal practices and norms within Brahmin communities and beyond.

7. Occupational Specialization:

While Brahmins were primarily associated with priestly duties and intellectual pursuits, they also engaged in various occupational roles and professions. Brahmins were involved in agriculture, trade, administration, and artisanal crafts, albeit to a lesser extent than other varnas.

However, their occupation was often secondary to their priestly duties and intellectual pursuits, reflecting the hierarchical nature of the caste system where certain occupations were deemed more prestigious than others.

While Brahmins were primarily associated with priestly duties, they also engaged in various occupations and professions. For instance, Charaka, an ancient Brahmin physician, is renowned for his contributions to Ayurveda, the traditional system of medicine in India. Charaka's treatise, the Charaka Samhita, remains a seminal text in Ayurvedic medicine, reflecting the Brahmin contribution to healthcare and healing arts.

8. Cultural Preservation and Innovation:

Brahmins have played a vital role in both

preserving and innovating cultural practices and traditions within Hindu society. Through their patronage of arts, literature, music, and dance, Brahmins have contributed to the enrichment and diversification of Indian culture. They have also been instrumental in adapting and synthesizing diverse cultural influences, fostering a dynamic and vibrant cultural landscape that reflects the synthesis of indigenous and foreign traditions.

Brahmins have played a vital role in preserving and innovating cultural practices and traditions. Kalidasa, a renowned Brahmin poet and playwright, is celebrated for his literary masterpieces such as the Shakuntala and Meghaduta. Kalidasa's works not only enriched Sanskrit literature but also showcased the artistic brilliance and creative imagination of Brahmin scholars, contributing to the cultural legacy of India.

9. Interactions with Other Castes:

Brahmins have had complex and nuanced interactions with other caste groups throughout history. While Brahmins held positions of authority and influence, they also depended on the patronage and support of other castes for their livelihoods. Brahmins engaged in reciprocal relationships with landowning castes, merchants, and rulers, exchanging spiritual services, knowledge, and material resources. These interactions were often characterized by both cooperation and conflict, reflecting the intricate social dynamics of the caste system.

Brahmins had complex interactions with other caste groups, characterized by cooperation and conflict. Ramanuja, a Brahmin theologian and philosopher, advocated for a more inclusive form of Hinduism that transcended caste distinctions. Ramanuja's teachings emphasized devotion (bhakti) to the divine as a path to salvation, welcoming people from all castes into the fold of Hindu spirituality and fostering greater social cohesion.

10. Contemporary Challenges and Debates:

In modern times, Brahmins continue to grapple with questions of identity, privilege, and social responsibility within the context of a rapidly changing society. Brahmins face criticism for perpetuating caste-based discrimination and inequality, while also confronting challenges to their traditional authority and status. Debates surrounding reservations, affirmative action, and caste-based politics have further complicated the role of Brahmins in contemporary Indian society, necessitating a nuanced understanding of their historical legacy and evolving social dynamics.

In contemporary India, Brahmins continue to navigate challenges related to caste dynamics and social change. B. R. Ambedkar, a prominent Dalit leader and social reformer who hailed from a Mahar caste background, challenged Brahminical hegemony and advocated for caste equality and social justice. Ambedkar's leadership in the Dalit movement and role in drafting the Indian Constitution reflect the ongoing debates and struggles surrounding caste identity and privilege in modern Indian society.

The role of Brahmins in the caste system is marked by a complex interplay of historical legacy, cultural influence, and contemporary dynamics. While Brahmins have historically wielded significant power and authority, their role in shaping caste relations and societal norms continues to evolve amidst ongoing debates and transformations in Indian society. Understanding the multifaceted nature of Brahmin influence within the caste system is essential for grappling with the complexities of caste dynamics and fostering greater social equity and inclusivity.

The misconceptions and criticisms surrounding Brahmins and caste discrimination

Brahmins, as a prominent social group in India, have been subject to various misconceptions and criticisms regarding their role in perpetuating caste discrimination. These misconceptions stem from historical realities, cultural stereotypes, and contemporary social dynamics, often oversimplifying the complexities of Brahmin identity and influence within the caste system. In this exploration, we delve into the nuanced nuances of the misconceptions and criticisms surrounding Brahmins and caste discrimination:

1. Perpetrators of Caste Discrimination:

One prevalent misconception is that all Brahmins are inherently responsible for perpetuating caste discrimination and inequality. While it is undeniable that Brahmins, as a privileged group within the caste system, have historically benefited from caste-based hierarchies, attributing sole responsibility to Brahmins overlooks the systemic nature of caste oppression. Caste discrimination is perpetuated by various factors, including social norms, economic disparities, and political structures, with complicity extending beyond any single caste group.

2. Monolithic Representation:

Another misconception is the tendency to homogenize Brahmins as a monolithic community, disregarding the diverse realities and experiences within the Brahmin population. Brahmins encompass a spectrum of socio-economic backgrounds, regional identities, and ideological beliefs, challenging the notion of a singular Brahmin identity. Painting all Brahmins with the same brush not only erases intra-caste differences but also perpetuates stereotypes that fail to capture the complexities of Brahmin lived experiences.

3. Blame for Historical Injustices:

Brahmins are often singled out and blamed for historical injustices and inequalities perpetuated under the caste system. While Brahmins held positions of privilege and authority in traditional society, attributing collective guilt to all Brahmins overlooks historical nuances and power dynamics. Caste discrimination is a deeply entrenched social phenomenon that implicates multiple caste groups, ruling elites, and socio-political institutions, requiring a nuanced understanding of historical complexities and inter-group dynamics.

4. Critique of Brahminical Hegemony:

Criticism of Brahmins often extends to the

concept of "Brahminical hegemony," wherein Brahmins are accused of imposing their cultural, religious, and social norms on other caste groups. This critique highlights power imbalances and cultural dominance within Indian society, where Brahminical narratives and values have historically held sway. However, it is essential to recognize that Brahminical hegemony is not a universal phenomenon and may vary across regions, communities, and historical periods.

5. Modern Reinterpretations and Rebuttals:

In response to these misconceptions and criticisms, scholars and activists have offered nuanced interpretations and rebuttals that challenge essentialist narratives and promote dialogue and understanding. Initiatives such as critical scholarship, social activism, and inter-caste solidarity movements seek to dismantle stereotypes, confront privilege, and foster inclusive narratives that acknowledge the complexities of caste dynamics and the role of all caste groups in perpetuating or challenging caste discrimination.

6. Economic Exploitation:

One aspect that often gets overlooked is the economic dimension of caste discrimination. While Brahmins may have held cultural and social privileges, the exploitation and marginalization of lower caste communities in economic spheres have been pervasive. The economic disparities perpetuated by the caste system have contributed to entrenched inequalities, with Brahmins often benefiting from inherited wealth and social networks.

7. Resistance and Dissent within Brahmin Community:

It's important to acknowledge that not all Brahmins have been complicit in perpetuating caste discrimination. Throughout history, there have been Brahmins who have actively resisted caste-based oppression and discrimination, advocating for social reform and equality. Figures like Jyotirao Phule and B. R. Ambedkar, who hailed from Brahmin backgrounds, challenged Brahminical orthodoxy and fought for the rights of marginalized castes.

8. Intersectionality and Multiple Identities:

Brahmins, like individuals from any social group, have multifaceted identities that intersect with factors such as gender, class, region, and religion. Recognizing the intersectionality of identities is crucial for understanding the diverse experiences and perspectives within the Brahmin community and how they navigate issues of caste discrimination. This nuanced approach avoids oversimplification and acknowledges the complexity of social realities.

Unraveling the misconceptions and criticisms surrounding Brahmins and caste discrimination requires a nuanced analysis that acknowledges historical realities, challenges essentialist narratives, and fosters empathy and understanding across caste lines. By interrogating stereotypes, deconstructing power dynamics, and amplifying marginalized voices, we can strive towards a more inclusive and equitable society that transcends caste-based divisions and fosters genuine solidarity and social justice.

The role of Brahmins in the caste system has been a subject of much debate and scrutiny, often shrouded in myths, stereotypes, and misconceptions. To understand the truth behind the Brahmin's role in the caste system, it is essential to delve into historical realities, socio-cultural contexts, and nuanced perspectives that go beyond simplistic narratives. Let us embark on a journey to unravel the truths behind the Brahmin's role in the caste system:

1. Historical Origins and Evolution:

The caste system, with its hierarchical social structure, emerged over centuries of socio-cultural evolution in ancient India. Brahmins, as the priestly class entrusted with religious duties and spiritual guidance, occupied a revered position within this system. However, the caste system was not static; it evolved over time, shaped by socio-economic changes, political dynamics, and religious beliefs. Brahmins played a significant role in codifying and perpetuating caste norms and customs through religious scriptures, rituals, and social institutions.

2. Guardians of Knowledge and Culture:

Brahmins were traditionally entrusted with the preservation and dissemination of knowledge, culture, and religious practices in Hindu society. They served as educators, scholars, and custodians of sacred texts, imparting spiritual wisdom and moral guidance to the community. Brahmins' role in transmitting cultural heritage and upholding traditional values contributed to their perceived authority and influence within the caste system.

3. Social Privilege and Power Dynamics:

While Brahmins held positions of privilege and authority in traditional society, it is essential to recognize that caste dynamics were characterized by complex power structures and inter-group relations. Brahmins' social status was often intertwined with patronage from ruling elites, landowning castes, and merchant communities. Economic factors, political alliances, and regional variations also influenced Brahmins' socio-economic standing and interactions with other caste groups.

4. Perpetuation and Resistance:

Brahmins, like individuals from any social

group, exhibited a range of attitudes and behaviors towards the caste system. While some Brahmins perpetuated caste-based discrimination and inequality, others challenged Brahminical orthodoxy and advocated for social reform. Figures like Raja Ram Mohan Roy and Swami Vivekananda questioned caste norms and worked towards social equality and religious harmony, showcasing the diversity of perspectives within the Brahmin community.

5. Contemporary Realities and Challenges:

In modern times, Brahmins continue to navigate complex socio-political landscapes marked by caste-based disparities, affirmative action policies, and identity politics. Brahmins face critiques for their historical privileges and responsibilities, as well as challenges to their traditional authority and status. Debates surrounding reservation policies, caste-based politics, and social justice initiatives reflect the ongoing tensions and complexities of Brahmins' role in contemporary Indian society.

6. Intellectual and Cultural Contributions:

Brahmins have made significant contributions to various fields, including literature, philosophy, science, and the arts, shaping India's intellectual and cultural heritage. Their scholarship and creativity have enriched society and transcended caste boundaries, fostering a shared cultural legacy that extends beyond caste divisions.

7. Regional and Community Variations:

It's important to acknowledge that Brahmins are not a homogenous group, and their roles and interactions within the caste system may vary based on regional, linguistic, and community-specific factors. Different Brahmin sub-castes and communities have distinct histories, traditions, and social dynamics that influence their relationship with the caste system.

8. Influence on Social Reform Movements:

Throughout history, Brahmins have played pivotal roles in social reform movements aimed at challenging caste discrimination and promoting social equality. Figures like Mahatma Jyotirao Phule and Periyar E. V. Ramasamy, who hailed from Brahmin backgrounds, led grassroots movements advocating for the rights of marginalized castes and communities, demonstrating the diverse responses within the Brahmin community to caste-based injustices.

9. Intersectionality and Gender Dynamics:

Exploring the intersectionality of caste and gender is crucial for understanding the complexities of the Brahmin's role in the caste system. Brahmin women, while sharing in the privileges and responsibilities of Brahmin identity, also face unique challenges and experiences shaped by gender norms, patriarchy, and caste dynamics. Their voices and perspectives contribute to a more nuanced understanding of Brahmin identity and its intersections with caste and gender.

10. Contemporary Dialogues and Reinterpretations:

In contemporary discourse, there is a growing emphasis on reinterpreting Brahmin identity and its relationship with the caste system in light of changing social realities and evolving perspectives.

Scholars, activists, and intellectuals engage in critical dialogues and debates to challenge stereotypes, interrogate power dynamics, and promote social justice, fostering a more inclusive and equitable society for all.

The truth behind the Brahmin's role in the caste system is multifaceted, encompassing historical legacies, cultural influences, and individual agency. By acknowledging the complexities and nuances of Brahmin identity and caste dynamics, we can strive towards a more nuanced understanding of the caste system and work towards fostering inclusive and equitable societies.

Chapter 6: The Brahmin and Education

The relationship between Brahmins and education has been intertwined throughout history, forming a cornerstone of Brahmin identity and cultural heritage. From ancient times to the present day, Brahmins have been revered as custodians of knowledge, entrusted with the transmission of wisdom, values, and traditions to successive generations.

Education has been central to Brahmin identity, with scriptures like the Vedas and Upanishads emphasizing the pursuit of knowledge as a sacred duty. Brahmins, as the priestly class, were responsible for studying, interpreting, and disseminating these sacred texts, fostering a culture of intellectual inquiry and spiritual exploration. Their role as educators and mentors extended beyond religious teachings to encompass a wide array of disciplines, including philosophy, grammar, mathematics, and astronomy.

Moreover, Brahmins have played a pivotal role in shaping educational institutions and systems, from ancient gurukuls to modern universities. Their emphasis on rigorous scholarship, critical thinking, and moral development has left an indelible mark on Indian education, influencing pedagogical approaches, curriculum design, and academic discourse. Through this exploration, we seek to unravel the intricate relationship between Brahmins and education, illuminating the enduring legacy of intellectual pursuit and cultural stewardship that continues to resonate in contemporary society.

The historical significance of education in Brahmin culture

Education holds profound significance in Brahmin culture, dating back to ancient times when Brahmins were entrusted with the sacred duty of preserving and disseminating knowledge. This historical significance is deeply rooted in the foundational texts of Hinduism, such as the Vedas and Upanishads, which extol the virtues of learning and wisdom. Let us embark on a journey through history to explore the rich tapestry of education in Brahmin culture:

1. Custodians of Sacred Knowledge:

Brahmins have long been regarded as the custodians of sacred knowledge, tasked with studying and interpreting the Vedas, the oldest scriptures of Hinduism. Through rigorous study and oral tradition, Brahmin scholars meticulously preserved the wisdom contained within these texts, ensuring its transmission from generation to generation. This sacred duty underscored the foundational role of education in Brahmin culture, elevating learning to a spiritual pursuit imbued with divine significance.

2. Gurukul Tradition:

The gurukul system, characterized by the residential schooling of students under the guidance of a guru (teacher), played a pivotal role in Brahmin education during ancient times. Young Brahmins would undergo rigorous training in gurukuls, where they would study not only religious texts but also a wide range of subjects, including philosophy, grammar, mathematics, and astronomy. This holistic approach to education fostered intellectual growth, moral development, and character formation, shaping the minds of future leaders and scholars.

3. Influence on Social Structure:

Education conferred social status and prestige upon Brahmins, elevating them to positions of authority and influence within society. As the learned elite, Brahmins held sway over religious rituals, philosophical discourse, and intellectual pursuits, wielding cultural power that transcended political boundaries. Their expertise in matters of religion, ethics, and governance shaped social norms, ethical codes, and moral values, leaving an indelible mark on the fabric of Hindu society.

4. Legacy of Scholarship and Innovation:

Brahmins have made enduring contributions to scholarship and intellectual inquiry, advancing knowledge in various fields and disciplines. From ancient sages like Vyasa and Valmiki to medieval philosophers like Adi Shankaracharya and Ramanuja, Brahmin intellectuals have enriched Hindu thought with their philosophical insights, theological debates, and literary creations. Their legacy of scholarship and innovation continues to inspire generations of scholars and seekers, fueling a tradition of intellectual curiosity and spiritual exploration.

5. Cultural Revival and Renaissance:

During periods of cultural revival and renaissance, Brahmins played instrumental roles in revitalizing education and fostering intellectual growth. Figures like Raja Ram Mohan Roy and Swami Vivekananda, who hailed from Brahmin backgrounds, championed educational reform, social justice, and religious tolerance, catalyzing transformative movements that reshaped Indian society. Their advocacy for modern education, scientific inquiry, and social equality reflected a commitment to progressive ideals rooted in the ethos of Brahmin culture.

The historical significance of education in Brahmin culture is a testament to the enduring legacy of knowledge and enlightenment that has shaped the intellectual landscape of India for millennia.

From the sanctity of ancient scriptures to the vibrancy of contemporary scholarship, education remains a cornerstone of Brahmin identity, embodying the quest for truth, wisdom, and spiritual liberation.

The impact of Brahmin scholars and their contributions to various fields

Throughout history, Brahmin scholars have made indelible contributions to various fields, enriching human understanding and advancing intellectual discourse. Their legacy of scholarship spans across disciplines, from philosophy and theology to science, literature, and the arts. Let us delve into the profound impact of Brahmin scholars and their contributions to diverse realms of knowledge:

1. Philosophy and Theology:

Brahmin scholars have been instrumental in shaping philosophical thought and theological discourse in India. Ancient philosophers like Adi Shankaracharya and Ramanuja revolutionized Hindu philosophy, establishing schools of thought that continue to influence religious doctrine and spiritual practice. Their dialectical debates, philosophical treatises, and commentaries on sacred texts elucidated complex metaphysical concepts and ethical principles, fostering intellectual inquiry and spiritual enlightenment.

2. Literature and Poetry:

Brahmin poets and writers have enriched Indian literature with their lyrical verses, epic narratives, and poetic compositions. Renowned figures like Valmiki, Vyasa, and Kalidasa have left an indelible mark on literary history with their timeless works such as the Ramayana, Mahabharata, and Shakuntala. Their literary masterpieces transcend linguistic boundaries, embodying the richness of Indian cultural heritage and the depth of human experience.

3. Science and Mathematics:

Brahmin scholars have made significant contributions to scientific inquiry and mathematical discovery, pioneering advancements in fields such as astronomy, medicine, and mathematics. Ancient astronomers like Aryabhata and Bhaskaracharya formulated groundbreaking theories of planetary motion and calculated accurate astronomical constants, laying the foundations for modern astronomy. Mathematicians like Brahmagupta and Bhaskara II made seminal discoveries in algebra, trigonometry, and calculus, shaping the development of mathematical thought in India and beyond.

4. Arts and Aesthetics:

Brahmin artists and aestheticians have played a vital role in fostering artistic expression and cultural innovation. From classical music maestros like Tyagaraja and Muthuswami Dikshitar to dance virtuosos like Bharatnatyam exponent Balasaraswati, Brahmin performers have elevated the performing arts to sublime heights with their mastery and devotion. Their creative genius, refined sensibility, and spiritual resonance have enriched the cultural tapestry of India, transcending temporal and spatial boundaries.

5. Social Reform and Activism:

Brahmin scholars have not only excelled in

intellectual pursuits but also demonstrated a commitment to social reform and activism. Visionaries like Raja Ram Mohan Roy and Swami Vivekananda challenged social injustices, advocated for human rights, and promoted religious tolerance, catalyzing transformative movements that reshaped Indian society. Their advocacy for education, gender equality, and social justice reflected a progressive ethos grounded in the principles of Brahminical ethics and compassion.

6. Linguistics and Grammar:

Brahmin scholars have made significant contributions to the field of linguistics and grammar, advancing theories of phonetics, morphology, and syntax. Figures like Panini, the ancient Sanskrit grammarian, formulated comprehensive grammatical rules and linguistic principles in his seminal work, the Ashtadhyayi. Panini's grammatical framework laid the foundation for the study of language and morphology, influencing subsequent developments in linguistic theory.

7. Medicine and Healthcare:

Brahmin physicians and medical practitioners have played a crucial role in the development of traditional Indian medicine systems such as Ayurveda. Notable physicians like Charaka and Sushruta authored foundational texts on Ayurvedic medicine, outlining principles of diagnosis, treatment, and pharmacology. Their contributions to medical science encompassed diverse fields, including herbal medicine, surgery, and holistic healing practices, shaping the foundations of holistic healthcare in India.

8. Political Thought and Governance:

Brahmin scholars have contributed to the realm of political thought and governance, offering insights into principles of statecraft, ethics, and governance. Figures like Kautilya (Chanakya), the ancient political theorist and strategist, authored the Arthashastra, a seminal treatise on statecraft, diplomacy, and political economy. Kautilya's pragmatic approach to governance and strategic thinking influenced political leaders and policymakers throughout history, offering timeless lessons in leadership and administration.

9. Environmental Conservation and Ecology:

Brahmin scholars have demonstrated a deep reverence for nature and a commitment to environmental conservation. Traditional texts like the

Vedas and Upanishads contain hymns and verses that extol the sanctity of nature and advocate for sustainable living practices. Brahmin environmentalists and ecologists have drawn inspiration from these teachings to promote ecological awareness, conservation efforts, and sustainable development initiatives, highlighting the holistic worldview of Brahminical philosophy.

10. Interdisciplinary Contributions:

Brahmin scholars have often bridged disciplinary boundaries, synthesizing insights from multiple fields to address complex challenges and societal issues. Interdisciplinary endeavors, such as the integration of philosophy with science, art, and ethics, have yielded innovative approaches to understanding the human condition and fostering holistic well-being.

Brahmin intellectuals continue to explore intersections between diverse disciplines, fostering interdisciplinary dialogue and collaboration in pursuit of knowledge and enlightenment.

The impact of Brahmin scholars transcends disciplinary boundaries, encompassing a diverse array of fields and endeavors. Their intellectual legacy continues to inspire generations of thinkers, innovators, and seekers, fostering a culture of learning, inquiry, and enlightenment that resonates across time and space.

The current state of education among Brahmins and the challenges they face

In contemporary times, the education landscape among Brahmins reflects both continuity with historical traditions and adaptation to modern realities. While Brahmins continue to place a high value on education and intellectual pursuits, they also grapple with a myriad of challenges that shape their educational experiences and opportunities. Let's explore the current state of education among Brahmins and the challenges they face:

1. Access and Affordability:

Despite a cultural emphasis on education, Brahmins, like many other communities, face challenges related to access and affordability. Economic disparities, regional disparities, and social barriers can hinder access to quality educational opportunities, particularly for those from marginalized or economically disadvantaged backgrounds. Limited access to educational resources, including schools, colleges, and vocational training centers, can perpetuate inequalities and hinder educational attainment.

2. Competition and Performance Pressure:

Brahmin students often face intense competition and performance pressure within educational systems characterized by merit-based evaluations and standardized testing without any fixed reservation allotment. The pursuit of academic excellence and career success can create immense pressure to excel academically, leading to stress, anxiety, and mental health challenges among students. High expectations from family, peers, and society can exacerbate these pressures, contributing to a culture of academic competitiveness and performance-oriented education.

3. Reservation Policies and Affirmative

Action:

Reservation policies and affirmative action initiatives aimed at promoting social equity and inclusion pose unique challenges for Brahmin students, particularly in contexts where reservation quotas are implemented in educational institutions and government jobs. Brahmins, who historically held privileged positions within the caste system, may perceive reservation policies as discriminatory or unfair, leading to feelings of resentment, frustration, and marginalization. These policies can also create tensions and inter-group conflicts within educational institutions and broader society.

4. Socio-cultural Dynamics and Identity:

Education among Brahmins is influenced by socio-cultural dynamics and identity considerations that shape educational choices, aspirations, and experiences. Cultural values, family expectations, and community norms play a significant role in shaping educational trajectories and career pathways for Brahmin students. The preservation of Brahminical traditions, religious teachings, and cultural heritage often intersects with educational goals, fostering a sense of identity and belonging within educational environments.

5. Modernization and Technological Integration:

As educational systems undergo rapid modernization and technological integration, Brahmin students must adapt to new learning modalities, digital platforms, and information technologies. While advancements in educational technology offer opportunities for enhanced learning experiences and access to global knowledge networks, they also pose challenges related to digital literacy, information overload, and cyber risks. Bridging the digital divide and ensuring equitable access to technology-based learning resources is crucial for promoting inclusive education among Brahmins and other communities.

6. Career Aspirations and Employment Opportunities:

Brahmin students navigate diverse career aspirations and employment opportunities in an increasingly competitive and dynamic job market. While traditional professions such as teaching, priesthood, and scholarly pursuits continue to attract youth, there is also a growing interest in non-traditional fields such as technology, entrepreneurship, and professional services. However, Brahmins may encounter challenges related to job market saturation, skill misalignment, and discrimination in employment practices, necessitating continuous skill development and career adaptation.

7. Social Stigma and Stereotypes:

Brahmins may encounter social stigma and stereotypes associated with their caste identity, which can manifest in various forms of discrimination, prejudice, and bias within educational settings. Stereotypes portraying Brahmins as privileged or elitist may lead to misconceptions about their academic achievements, abilities, and aspirations, impacting their social interactions, self-esteem, and sense of belonging within educational institutions.

8. Language and Cultural Preservation:

Brahmins may face challenges related to

language and cultural preservation in educational contexts where there is a dominant emphasis on mainstream languages and cultures. The preservation of Sanskrit, classical literature, and indigenous knowledge systems may be overlooked or marginalized within educational curricula, posing challenges for students seeking to engage with their linguistic and cultural heritage.

9. Intersectional Identities and Diversity:

Brahmins encompass a diverse range of identities and experiences beyond their caste affiliation, including gender, class, religion, and regional backgrounds. Intersectional identities intersect with educational experiences and outcomes, shaping access to opportunities, resources, and support systems. Recognizing the diversity within the Brahmin community and addressing the intersecting dimensions of identity is essential for promoting inclusivity and equity in education.

10. Community Empowerment and Collective Action:

Addressing challenges in education among Brahmins requires collective action and community empowerment initiatives that prioritize collaboration, advocacy, and capacity-building. Community-based organizations, educational institutions, and civil society groups can play a crucial role in fostering dialogue, awareness, and solidarity among Brahmins and other marginalized communities, advocating for policy reforms, and providing support services to address educational disparities.

The current state of education among

Brahmins reflects a complex interplay of socio-economic, cultural, and institutional factors that shape educational outcomes and opportunities. By addressing these challenges and fostering an inclusive and equitable educational environment, Brahmins can continue to uphold their legacy of scholarship, intellectual inquiry, and service to society in the modern era.

Chapter 7: The Brahmin and Religion

The intersection of Brahmin identity and religion forms a cornerstone of Indian culture, spirituality, and social organization. Brahmins, traditionally designated as the priestly class within Hindu society, play a pivotal role in preserving, propagating, and practicing religious rituals, ceremonies, and teachings.

Brahmins have historically served as intermediaries between humanity and the divine, mediating religious rituals, offering spiritual guidance, and interpreting scriptures to facilitate individuals' spiritual journeys. Their deep-rooted connection to Vedic texts, Puranic literature, and philosophical treatises underscores their role as guardians of ancient wisdom and custodians of religious traditions passed down through generations.

Brahmins have contributed to the preservation and evolution of Hinduism, India's predominant religious tradition, through their scholarship, theological insights, and ritual expertise. Their adherence to religious principles, ethical conduct, and ascetic practices exemplifies a commitment to spiritual purity and moral integrity that permeates Brahminical ethos.

Through this exploration, we seek to unravel the intricate tapestry of Brahminical religiosity, shedding light on its enduring significance in shaping religious discourse, cultural identity, and social cohesion within Indian society.

Brahmins have played a pivotal role in preserving and propagating Hinduism, India's oldest and most pervasive religious tradition. Rooted in ancient scriptures, rituals, and philosophical teachings, Hinduism encompasses a diverse array of beliefs, practices, and cultural expressions that have been safeguarded and transmitted through generations by Brahmin scholars, priests, and spiritual leaders. Let's explore the multifaceted role of Brahmins in preserving and propagating Hinduism:

1. Guardians of Sacred Knowledge:

Brahmins have served as custodians of sacred knowledge, meticulously preserving and transmitting Vedic scriptures, Puranic texts, and philosophical treatises through oral tradition and scriptural study. Their expertise in Sanskrit language and literature has enabled them to interpret, recite, and disseminate sacred texts, ensuring the continuity and authenticity of Hindu religious teachings.

2. Ritual Experts and Spiritual Guides:

Brahmins have been entrusted with the performance of religious rituals, ceremonies, and sacraments prescribed in Hindu scriptures. As priests (purohits) and ritual specialists (pandits), they conduct elaborate rituals such as yagnas (fire sacrifices), pujas (worship ceremonies), and sanskaras (sacraments) for individuals, families, and communities, facilitating spiritual communion with divine forces and fostering auspiciousness in life.

3. Interpreters of Religious Texts:

Brahmins play a vital role in interpreting and elucidating the meaning of Hindu scriptures, offering insights into theological concepts, moral precepts, and philosophical doctrines. Through commentaries (bhashyas), discourses (pravachanas), and theological debates (shastrartha), Brahmin scholars engage in intellectual discourse, theological inquiry, and scriptural exegesis, enriching the understanding of Hindu religious thought and doctrine.

4. Spiritual and Moral Exemplars:

Brahmins embody the ideals of dharma (righteousness), ahimsa (non-violence), and self-discipline, serving as moral exemplars and spiritual role models within Hindu society. Their adherence to religious principles, ethical conduct, and ascetic practices inspires reverence and emulation among devotees, fostering a culture of piety, virtue, and spiritual awakening.

5. Cultural Stewards and Community Leaders:

Brahmins contribute to the preservation and promotion of Hindu culture, arts, and traditions, serving as cultural stewards and community leaders. They oversee temple administration, religious festivals, and cultural events, fostering a sense of communal solidarity and religious identity among Hindu communities. Moreover, Brahmins provide spiritual counsel, guidance, and support to individuals seeking solace, guidance, and spiritual upliftment.

6. Educational Institutions and Gurukuls:

Brahmins have historically established and

maintained educational institutions, known as gurukuls or vedic schools, where students receive instruction in Vedic scriptures, religious rituals, and philosophical teachings. These gurukuls serve as centers of learning and spiritual initiation, fostering the transmission of knowledge from guru (teacher) to shishya (student) in a traditional guru-shishya parampara (teacher-disciple lineage).

7. Scriptural Commentaries and Expositions:

Brahmin scholars have authored numerous commentaries, expositions, and theological treatises elucidating Hindu scriptures and philosophical texts. These scholarly works provide in-depth analysis, interpretation, and application of religious teachings, helping to clarify doctrinal ambiguities, resolve theological debates, and deepen spiritual understanding among practitioners.

8. Social Welfare and Humanitarian Initiatives:

Brahmins have engaged in charitable activities, philanthropic endeavors, and social welfare initiatives aimed at alleviating human suffering, promoting social justice, and uplifting marginalized communities. Through acts of seva (selfless service), dana (charity), and bhiksha (alms-giving), Brahmins embody the spirit of compassion, generosity, and empathy prescribed in Hindu scriptures, contributing to the welfare of society at large.

9. Cultural Revival and Renaissance Movements:

Brahmins have played significant roles in cultural revival and renaissance movements aimed at revitalizing Hindu culture, arts, and spirituality during periods of social and political upheaval. Visionaries and reformers from Brahmin backgrounds have spearheaded movements to promote linguistic revival, cultural preservation, and religious reform, revitalizing Hindu traditions and fostering a sense of cultural pride and identity.

10. Interfaith Dialogue and Religious Harmony:

Brahmins have contributed to interfaith dialogue, religious tolerance, and ecumenical cooperation, fostering mutual understanding and harmony among diverse religious communities. Through interfaith initiatives, ecumenical gatherings, and dialogue forums, Brahmin leaders seek to promote peace, coexistence, and respect for religious diversity, embodying the universal values of tolerance, pluralism, and coexistence inherent in Hinduism.

The role of Brahmins in preserving and propagating Hinduism is multifaceted, encompassing spiritual, cultural, and social dimensions. Their dedication to sacred knowledge, ritual expertise, moral integrity, and community service underscores their indispensable contribution to the continuity and vitality of Hindu religious traditions.

The rituals and ceremonies performed by Brahmins

Brahmins, as the priestly class in Hindu society, play a central role in performing a wide array of rituals and ceremonies that are integral to the religious and cultural fabric of Hinduism. Rooted in ancient scriptures, Vedic injunctions, and Puranic traditions, these rituals and ceremonies serve diverse purposes, ranging from invoking divine blessings to marking life transitions and propitiating celestial forces. Let's delve into the rich tapestry of rituals and ceremonies performed by Brahmins:

1. Yagnas and Homa:

Yagnas, also known as fire sacrifices, are elaborate ritual ceremonies performed by Brahmins to invoke celestial deities and appease cosmic forces through offerings into the sacred fire (agni). These rituals, prescribed in Vedic texts, involve intricate rituals, chanting of mantras, and recitation of Vedic hymns to seek blessings for prosperity, health, and spiritual growth. Homa, a simplified version of yagnas, involves offerings into the sacred fire accompanied by specific chants and prayers for specific purposes.

2. Pujas and Worship Ceremonies:

Pujas, or worship ceremonies, are ritualistic acts of devotion performed by Brahmins and householders to honor and propitiate deities, gods, and goddesses. These ceremonies involve offerings of flowers, fruits, incense, and other sacred items to the deity's image or idol, accompanied by the recitation of prayers, hymns, and mantras. Pujas are performed daily, on auspicious occasions, and during religious festivals to cultivate spiritual devotion and seek divine blessings for well-being and prosperity.

3. Sanskaras and Life-cycle Rituals:

Sanskaras, or sacraments, are a series of

life-cycle rituals performed by Brahmins to mark significant milestones and transitions in an individual's life journey. These rituals include ceremonies such as Namkaran (naming ceremony), Annaprashan (first feeding of solid food), Upanayana (sacred thread ceremony), Vivaha (marriage ceremony), and Antyeshti (funeral rites). Sanskaras are designed to imbue life's passages with spiritual significance, cultural symbolism, and ethical values, ensuring the continuity of religious traditions and familial legacies.

4. Shraddha and Ancestor Worship:

Shraddha, or ancestral rites, are rituals performed by Brahmins to honor and propitiate ancestors (pitris) for their blessings and guidance. These ceremonies, conducted on specific days according to the lunar calendar or during the Pitru Paksha period, involve offerings of food, water, and prayers to deceased ancestors, accompanied by rituals to ensure their spiritual welfare and liberation. Ancestor worship reflects the belief in the continuity of familial bonds and the importance of honoring one's lineage and heritage.

5. Temple Rituals and Festivals:

Brahmins serve as priests in Hindu temples, where they perform daily rituals (nitya karmas) and festive ceremonies (utsavas) to worship and serve the deity residing in the sanctum sanctorum. Temple rituals include practices such as Abhishekam (ceremonial bathing of the deity), Alankaram (decorating the deity), Arati (offering of lights), and Kirtan (devotional singing). Festivals like Navaratri, Diwali, and Shivaratri are celebrated with elaborate rituals, processions, and cultural performances, showcasing the vibrancy of Hindu religious traditions.

6. Samskaras (Sacraments):

Brahmins are responsible for conducting various samskaras or sacraments throughout the life cycle of an individual, marking significant milestones and transitions. These include ceremonies such as Garbhadhana (conception), Pumsavana (pregnancy announcement), Simantonnayana (baby shower), Jatakarma (birth rites), Namakarana (naming ceremony), Annaprashana (first solid feeding), Chudakarana (tonsure), Upanayana (thread ceremony), Vivaha (marriage), and Antyeshti (funeral rites). Each of these rituals is performed with precision and adherence to scriptural injunctions, ensuring spiritual sanctity and auspiciousness.

7. Festivals and Observances:

Brahmins play a central role in the celebration and observance of Hindu festivals and religious occasions, organizing and conducting elaborate rituals, pujas, and homas (fire sacrifices) associated with these festivities. From major festivals such as Diwali, Navaratri, and Holi to regional celebrations like Pongal, Onam, and Durga Puja, Brahmins serve as priests, officiants, and facilitators of religious rituals, ensuring the sanctity and efficacy of the observances.

8. Temple Worship and Puja:

Brahmins are entrusted with the responsibility of performing worship (puja) and offering rituals (archana) at temples dedicated to various deities. As temple priests (pujaris), they conduct daily rituals, abhishekams (ablutions), alankaras (decoration), and aratis (ritualistic offerings) to appease the divine presiding deity and facilitate devotees' spiritual communion. Brahmins follow intricate procedures and protocols prescribed in Agamic texts and temple traditions, maintaining the sanctity and purity of temple worship.

9. Vratas and Upavasas (Fasting Observances):

Brahmins observe vratas (vows) and upavasas (fasts) on auspicious days dedicated to specific deities or celestial occurrences. These fasting observances are accompanied by special rituals, prayers, and recitations of sacred texts, aimed at invoking divine blessings, purifying the body and mind, and cultivating spiritual discipline. Brahmins guide devotees in observing vratas and upavasas, providing spiritual guidance and support throughout the fasting period.

10. Esoteric and Tantric Rituals:

In addition to mainstream rituals and ceremonies, Brahmins also perform esoteric and tantric rituals associated with specialized forms of worship, meditation, and spiritual practice. These rituals may involve elaborate yantra puja (worship of geometric diagrams), mantra japa (recitation of sacred chants), and tantra sadhana (ritualistic practices) aimed at invoking divine energies, attaining spiritual enlightenment, and unlocking occult powers. Brahmins trained in tantra shastras (scriptures) undertake these rituals with utmost secrecy and adherence to traditional methods.

The rituals and ceremonies performed by

Brahmins embody the timeless wisdom, spiritual fervor, and cultural heritage of Hinduism, serving as sacred conduits for divine communion, ethical transformation, and communal solidarity within Hindu society.

The misconceptions surrounding Brahmins and their religious practices

Misconceptions surrounding Brahmins and their religious practices often stem from oversimplifications or misinterpretations of their roles within Hindu society. Addressing these misconceptions requires a nuanced understanding of Brahminical traditions and the diverse ways in which they manifest in religious rituals and ceremonies. Let's delve into some common misconceptions and provide clarity on Brahmins and their religious practices:

1. Monolithic Representation:

One prevalent misconception is the notion of Brahmins as a monolithic group with uniform religious practices. In reality, Brahmins comprise a diverse community with regional variations, sectarian affiliations, and individual differences in religious observance. While certain rituals and ceremonies may be common among Brahmins, there is considerable diversity in the interpretation and performance of religious rites across different Brahmin communities.

2. Exclusivity and Elitism:

Another misconception is the perception of Brahminical rituals as exclusive or elitist, reserved solely for Brahmins and inaccessible to other castes or communities. While Brahmins often officiate in religious ceremonies and perform priestly duties,

Hindu scriptures emphasize inclusivity and openness in religious participation. Non-Brahmins, irrespective of caste or social status, can actively engage in religious rituals and seek spiritual guidance from Brahmin priests.

3. Ritual Rigidity and Orthodoxy:

There is a misconception that Brahminical rituals are rigidly prescribed and bound by orthodoxy, resistant to change or adaptation. While certain core rituals may adhere to traditional norms and scriptural injunctions, Brahminical practices have evolved over time in response to societal changes, cultural influences, and theological developments. Brahmin priests demonstrate flexibility in adapting rituals to contemporary contexts while upholding the essence of tradition.

4. Ritualistic Superstition:

Some misconceptions portray Brahminical rituals as mere acts of superstition devoid of deeper spiritual significance. In reality, Hindu rituals are imbued with symbolic meaning, spiritual intent, and philosophical depth, reflecting cosmic principles and metaphysical truths. Brahmin priests are trained in the symbolism and philosophy underlying rituals, guiding devotees in understanding their spiritual significance and fostering deeper engagement with religious practices.

5. Caste Discrimination in Rituals:

There is a misconception that Brahminical rituals perpetuate caste discrimination or hierarchy, excluding lower castes from participation or marginalizing their involvement. While historical instances of caste-based exclusion may exist, contemporary Brahminical practices prioritize inclusivity, equality, and universal access to religious rites. Brahmin priests often officiate in ceremonies for individuals from diverse backgrounds, emphasizing the universality of spiritual teachings and the sanctity of human dignity.

6. Economic Exploitation:

Another misconception suggests that Brahmin priests exploit their privileged position to extract economic benefits or material offerings from devotees. While priests may receive dakshina (offerings) as a customary gesture of gratitude, the exchange is symbolic rather than transactional, emphasizing reciprocity and mutual respect between priest and devotee. Brahmin priests uphold ethical conduct and integrity in their interactions with devotees, fostering trust and authenticity in religious rituals.

7. Homogeneity of Beliefs and Practices:

One common misconception is the assumption of homogeneity among Brahmins regarding their religious beliefs and practices. In reality, Brahmins represent a diverse spectrum of beliefs, sects, and regional variations within Hinduism. While certain rituals and ceremonies may be common among Brahmins, there exists considerable diversity in the interpretation, performance, and adherence to religious practices based on factors such as lineage, community traditions, and individual preferences.

8. Exclusivity and Elitism:

Another misconception is the perception of Brahmins as exclusivist or elitist in their religious practices, excluding individuals from other caste groups or communities. While Brahmins may have traditionally held privileged roles in performing certain rituals or ceremonies, Hinduism emphasizes inclusivity and accessibility to spiritual practices for all individuals, regardless of caste or social status. Many rituals and ceremonies performed by Brahmins are open to participation by members of all castes, fostering a sense of community and religious unity.

9. Lack of Adaptability and Innovation:

There is a misconception that Brahmins adhere rigidly to ancient traditions and resist adaptation or innovation in their religious practices. However, Brahminical traditions have demonstrated remarkable adaptability and evolution over time, incorporating new rituals, customs, and interpretations in response to changing social, cultural, and religious contexts. Brahmins have continuously adapted their religious practices to accommodate diverse beliefs, technological advancements, and contemporary challenges while retaining core spiritual principles.

10. Monopoly on Spiritual Authority:

Another misconception is the perception of Brahmins as the sole arbiters of spiritual authority within Hinduism, monopolizing religious leadership roles and hierarchical structures. While Brahmins have historically held prominent positions as priests, scholars, and religious leaders, Hinduism recognizes the diversity of spiritual paths and the multiplicity of religious authorities beyond Brahminical traditions. Many non-Brahmin communities and sects within

Hinduism have their own religious leaders, gurus, and spiritual lineages, contributing to the pluralistic nature of Hindu religious landscape.

11. Inherent Purity or Superiority:

Finally, there is a misconception that Brahmins inherently possess spiritual purity or superiority by virtue of their birth or caste status. However, Hinduism emphasizes the importance of individual merit, ethical conduct, and spiritual practice over birth-based privileges. While Brahmins may undergo rigorous training and adhere to strict codes of conduct, their spiritual status is not determined solely by caste affiliation but by their adherence to dharma (righteousness) and pursuit of spiritual realization.

By dispelling these misconceptions and fostering a more nuanced understanding of Brahmins and their religious practices, we can promote dialogue, mutual respect, and cultural appreciation within diverse religious communities. Brahmins play a vital role as custodians of sacred knowledge, spiritual guides, and cultural stewards, enriching the tapestry of Hindu religious traditions and fostering spiritual harmony in society.

Chapter 8: The Brahmin and Politics

In the intricate tapestry of Indian society, the role of Brahmins in politics is both profound and complex, characterized by a rich legacy of intellectual leadership, ideological influence, and social activism. From ancient times to the contemporary era, Brahmins have wielded significant influence in shaping political discourse, governance structures, and societal values, contributing to the fabric of democratic governance and socio-political transformation. This exploration delves into the multifaceted relationship between Brahmins and politics, unraveling their historical contributions, contemporary challenges, and evolving roles within the political landscape of India.

Brahmins have historically occupied prominent positions of leadership and authority, serving as advisors to kings, administrators of kingdoms, and custodians of legal and ethical norms. Their erudition, ethical integrity, and commitment to dharma (righteousness) have earned them respect and admiration across generations, positioning them as trusted custodians of political power and moral authority.

Furthermore, Brahmins have played pivotal roles in shaping political ideologies, fostering social reform movements, and advocating for justice, equality, and human rights. Their intellectual prowess, moral conviction, and social consciousness have propelled them into the forefront of political activism, championing causes ranging from social justice and environmental conservation to minority rights and democratic governance.

Through this exploration, we seek to unravel the nuanced dynamics of Brahminical influence in politics, examining the intersections of power, ideology, and public service within the ever-evolving landscape of Indian democracy.

Across the annals of Indian history, Brahmins have played a significant role in shaping political structures, governance systems, and socio-cultural movements, leaving an indelible mark on the political landscape of the subcontinent. From ancient kingdoms to modern democracies, Brahmins have occupied diverse roles in politics, ranging from advisors and administrators to lawmakers and revolutionaries. Let's explore the multifaceted involvement of Brahmins in politics throughout history:

1. Advisors to Kings and Rulers:

Brahmins have served as trusted advisors and counselors to kings, emperors, and rulers in ancient Indian kingdoms. Endowed with wisdom, knowledge, and ethical discernment, Brahmin advisors provided guidance on matters of statecraft, diplomacy, and governance, shaping the policies and decisions of ruling dynasties. Their influence extended beyond political affairs to encompass moral and spiritual guidance, ensuring the alignment of political power with dharmic principles.

2. Administrators and Bureaucrats:

Brahmins held key administrative positions within ancient kingdoms and empires, serving as ministers, administrators, and bureaucrats responsible for the governance and management of state affairs. Their expertise in law, ethics, and governance facilitated the implementation of just and equitable policies, fostering stability and prosperity within their respective domains. Brahmin administrators played instrumental roles in maintaining law and order, overseeing public welfare initiatives, and resolving disputes through judicial arbitration.

3. Founders of Political Ideologies:

Brahmins have been pioneers in the formulation and dissemination of political ideologies and philosophies that have shaped the course of Indian history. Visionary thinkers and reformers like Chanakya (Kautilya), the author of the Arthashastra, articulated political theories and strategies that influenced governance practices and statecraft in ancient India. Their insights into principles of governance, leadership, and statecraft continue to resonate in contemporary political discourse.

4. Leaders of Social Reform Movements:

Throughout history, Brahmins have emerged as leaders of social reform movements aimed at addressing social injustices, inequalities, and systemic injustices within Indian society. Figures like Raja Ram Mohan Roy, Dayananda Saraswati, and Swami Vivekananda led movements advocating for social reforms, education, and women's rights, challenging caste-based discrimination, and promoting societal harmony and upliftment.

5. Revolutionary Figures and Freedom

Fighters:

Brahmins have actively participated in India's struggle for independence from colonial rule, contributing to the nationalist movement through acts of resistance, civil disobedience, and revolutionary activism. Leaders like Bal Gangadhar Tilak, Lala Lajpat Rai, and Bipin Chandra Pal played instrumental roles in mobilizing masses, organizing protests, and advocating for Swaraj (self-rule), inspiring generations of freedom fighters to challenge British colonial hegemony.

6. Political Leadership in Modern Democracies:

In contemporary times, Brahmins continue to occupy positions of political leadership and influence within the democratic framework of India. Many Brahmins have served as presidents, prime ministers, chief ministers, and parliamentarians, contributing to policy formulation, legislative debates, and governance at the national, state, and local levels. Their participation in electoral politics and public service reflects a commitment to democratic principles, public welfare, and nation-building.

7. Advocates for Social Justice and Equity:

Brahmins have been vocal advocates for social justice, equity, and inclusive development, advocating for policies and initiatives aimed at addressing socio-economic disparities, caste discrimination, and marginalized communities' empowerment. Through activism, advocacy, and community organizing, Brahmins have sought to promote egalitarian values, foster inter-caste harmony, and advance the cause of social reform in Indian society.

The involvement of Brahmins in politics throughout history reflects a rich tapestry of leadership, influence, and ideological diversity, underscoring their enduring legacy as stewards of political governance, social justice, and democratic ideals in the Indian subcontinent.

The influence of Brahmins in shaping political ideologies and policies

Throughout Indian history, Brahmins have wielded significant influence in shaping political ideologies and policies, contributing to the formulation of governance structures, socio-political movements, and ideological frameworks that have shaped the trajectory of Indian politics. Their intellectual acumen, moral authority, and commitment to dharma (righteousness) have positioned them as pivotal actors in political discourse, governance, and policy formulation. Let's delve into the multifaceted influence of Brahmins in shaping political ideologies and policies:

1. Ideological Pioneers:

Brahmins have been instrumental in formulating and disseminating political ideologies that have shaped the course of Indian history. Visionary thinkers and philosophers like Chanakya (Kautilya) laid the groundwork for political theory and statecraft through works such as the Arthashastra, which delineated principles of governance, diplomacy, and administration. Their insights into the nature of power, leadership, and governance continue to inform political thought and practice.

2. Advocates of Dharma and Social Justice:

Brahmins have advocated for governance based on principles of dharma (righteousness), justice, and ethical conduct. Inspired by dharmic principles embedded in Hindu scriptures, Brahmin intellectuals and leaders have championed causes such as social reform, equality, and the welfare of all segments of society. Their emphasis on moral integrity, compassion, and social responsibility has influenced political ideologies centered on social justice and inclusive development.

3. Custodians of Tradition and Culture:

Brahmins have played a crucial role in preserving and promoting traditional Indian culture, values, and heritage within the political sphere. Through their scholarship, cultural activism, and advocacy, Brahmins have sought to safeguard indigenous knowledge systems, artistic traditions, and religious practices, fostering a sense of cultural pride and identity among diverse communities. Their influence in shaping cultural policies and initiatives has contributed to the preservation and revitalization of India's rich cultural heritage.

4. Advocates of Spiritual Governance:

Brahmins have advocated for a holistic approach to governance that integrates spiritual values, ethical principles, and moral leadership. Drawing from Hindu philosophical traditions, Brahmin leaders have emphasized the importance of spiritual enlightenment, ethical conduct, and selfless service in the exercise of political power. Their advocacy for spiritual governance has influenced political ideologies that prioritize the well-being of individuals and communities over narrow partisan interests.

5. Architects of Reform Movements:

Brahmins have been at the forefront of reform movements aimed at challenging social injustices, caste-based discrimination, and systemic inequalities within Indian society. Figures like Raja Ram Mohan Roy, Dayananda Saraswati, and Mahatma Gandhi, all from Brahmin backgrounds, led movements advocating for social reform, education, and human rights. Their ideological leadership and grassroots mobilization efforts galvanized public support for transformative change, shaping the political landscape of India.

6. Intellectual Leadership in Modern Democracies:

In contemporary democracies, Brahmins continue to exert influence in shaping political ideologies and policies through intellectual leadership, policy advocacy, and public discourse. Brahmin intellectuals, academics, and policymakers contribute to policy formulation, legislative debates, and governance strategies, leveraging their expertise and insights to address contemporary challenges and chart a course for national development.

The influence of Brahmins in shaping political ideologies and policies reflects a convergence of intellectual rigor, moral conviction, and visionary leadership, underscoring their enduring legacy as architects of governance and ideological visionaries in the Indian political landscape.

In contemporary India, Brahmins continue to hold significant representation in politics, contributing to various political parties, governance structures, and policy-making processes. However, their political involvement is not without challenges, as they grapple with issues ranging from caste-based politics to perceptions of privilege and historical prejudices. Let's delve into the current representation of Brahmins in politics and the challenges they face:

1. Political Representation:

Brahmins have historically been well-represented in political leadership positions at both the national and state levels. Many prominent political figures from Brahmin backgrounds have served as presidents, prime ministers, chief ministers, and parliamentarians, contributing to policy formulation, legislative debates, and governance. However, the extent of Brahmin representation in politics varies across different regions and political parties.

2. Caste-Based Politics:

One of the primary challenges faced by Brahmins in politics is the prevalence of caste-based politics, wherein caste identities play a significant role in electoral dynamics, social mobilization, and coalition building. Brahmins, often perceived as belonging to the upper caste, may face backlash or criticism from other caste groups, leading to political polarization and identity-based voting patterns. This dynamic poses challenges for Brahmins seeking to build inclusive political alliances and foster social cohesion.

3. Perceptions of Privilege and Elitism:

Brahmins are sometimes viewed through the lens of historical privilege and elitism, stemming from their traditional roles as priests, scholars, and administrators in ancient Indian society. This perception can create barriers to political engagement and public trust, as Brahmins may be perceived as disconnected from the concerns and aspirations of marginalized communities. Overcoming these perceptions requires Brahmin leaders to demonstrate empathy, inclusivity, and a commitment to social justice in their political engagement.

4. Identity Politics and Marginalization:

In the context of identity politics, Brahmins may face marginalization or discrimination based on their caste identity, particularly in regions where anti-Brahmin sentiments are prevalent. Stereotypes and prejudices about Brahmins as oppressors or beneficiaries of caste privilege can hinder their political aspirations and leadership potential, creating barriers to equal representation and participation in democratic processes.

5. Challenges of Social Justice Advocacy:

Despite their historical contributions to social reform movements and advocacy for social justice, Brahmins may encounter skepticism or resistance when championing progressive policies or initiatives aimed at addressing caste-based discrimination, inequality, and social exclusion. Overcoming these challenges requires Brahmins to engage in meaningful dialogue, coalition-building, and allyship with marginalized communities, demonstrating a commitment to dismantling caste-based hierarchies and fostering inclusive development.

6. Opportunities for Leadership and Collaboration:

Despite the challenges they face, Brahmins have opportunities to contribute positively to politics by leveraging their intellectual leadership, policy expertise, and grassroots connections. By engaging in grassroots activism, community organizing, and advocacy for progressive policies, Brahmin leaders can build bridges across caste divides, promote social cohesion, and advance the cause of democratic governance.

The current representation of Brahmins in politics reflects a complex interplay of historical legacies, identity dynamics, and contemporary challenges. By addressing issues of caste-based politics, perceptions of privilege, and barriers to social justice advocacy, Brahmin leaders can play a constructive role in shaping inclusive and equitable political systems that uphold the principles of democracy, social justice, and pluralism.

Chapter 9: The Brahmin and Society

In the intricate tapestry of Indian society, the Brahmin community occupies a unique and multifaceted position, embodying a rich legacy of cultural stewardship, intellectual leadership, and social responsibility. From ancient times to the modern era, Brahmins have played pivotal roles in shaping the fabric of society through their contributions to diverse fields such as art, literature, education, and spirituality. This exploration delves into the multifaceted relationship between Brahmins and society, unraveling the intricacies of their historical legacy, contemporary challenges, and enduring impact on the social landscape of India.

Brahmins have long been revered as custodians of tradition, preserving and propagating ancient knowledge, cultural practices, and spiritual teachings passed down through generations. Their role as educators, scholars, and custodians of sacred texts has fostered a culture of learning and intellectual inquiry that has enriched Indian society for millennia. Moreover, Brahmins have been instrumental in shaping social norms, moral values, and ethical standards that form the foundation of a harmonious and virtuous society.

However, the Brahmin community also grapples with contemporary challenges and criticisms, ranging from accusations of elitism and privilege to concerns about caste-based discrimination and social inequality. By navigating these challenges with resilience, introspection, and a commitment to social justice, Brahmins continue to play a vital role in promoting cultural heritage, fostering intellectual growth, and advocating for inclusive development within Indian society.

The contributions of Brahmins to society in various fields such as art, literature, and science

Throughout history, Brahmins have made significant contributions to various fields, enriching society with their expertise, creativity, and intellectual prowess. Their impact spans diverse domains, including art, literature, science, and philosophy, shaping the cultural landscape of India and beyond. Let's explore the contributions of Brahmins to society in these fields:

1. Art and Aesthetics:

Brahmins have been instrumental in nurturing artistic traditions and aesthetic sensibilities in Indian society. From classical music and dance to sculpture and painting, Brahmin artists have excelled in diverse art forms, preserving ancient traditions and innovating new expressions. Figures like Tyagaraja, M.S. Subbulakshmi, and Raja Ravi Varma have left an indelible mark on Indian art and culture, inspiring generations with their creativity and artistic mastery.

2. Literature and Scholarship:

Brahmins have been prolific writers, poets, and scholars, contributing to the rich literary heritage of India in languages such as Sanskrit, Tamil, Telugu, and Kannada. From the Vedas and Upanishads to classical epics like the Mahabharata and Ramayana, Brahmin scholars have produced timeless literary works that explore profound philosophical themes, moral values, and human experiences. Figures like Kalidasa, Adi Shankaracharya, and Bharathiyaar have shaped literary traditions and intellectual discourse through their literary contributions.

3. Science and Philosophy:

Brahmins have played a significant role in advancing scientific knowledge and philosophical inquiry in ancient India. Through rigorous study and empirical observation, Brahmin scholars made groundbreaking discoveries in fields such as mathematics, astronomy, medicine, and metaphysics. Figures like Aryabhata, Sushruta, and Patanjali made pioneering contributions to scientific knowledge, laying the foundation for later advancements in science and technology.

4. Education and Knowledge Transmission:

Brahmins have been the custodians of knowledge and education in Indian society, serving as teachers, mentors, and guardians of wisdom. Through gurukuls (traditional schools) and vedic institutions, Brahmin educators imparted knowledge of scriptures, philosophy, literature, and practical skills to successive generations. Their dedication to learning and intellectual pursuit has nurtured a culture of scholarship and academic excellence in Indian society.

5. Social Reform and Advocacy:

Brahmins have been at the forefront of social reform movements aimed at challenging social injustices, caste-based discrimination, and inequality. Figures like Swami Vivekananda, Mahatma Phule, and Periyar E.V. Ramasamy advocated for social reform, education for all, and women's rights, challenging orthodox beliefs and advocating for social equality. Their efforts have contributed to the progress of Indian society and the advancement of human rights and social justice.

The contributions of Brahmins to society in various fields demonstrate their multifaceted legacy of creativity, intellect, and cultural enrichment. By nurturing artistic traditions, advancing knowledge, and advocating for social reform, Brahmins have left an indelible imprint on the cultural, intellectual, and social fabric of India, embodying the values of creativity, knowledge, and social responsibility.

Throughout history, Brahmins have played a crucial role in advocating for social welfare and equality, championing causes aimed at uplifting marginalized communities, combating caste-based discrimination, and promoting social justice. Their commitment to dharma (righteousness), compassion, and service to humanity has driven initiatives that address societal inequities and foster inclusive development. Let's delve into the multifaceted role of Brahmins in promoting social welfare and equality:

1. Advocacy for Social Reform:

Brahmins have been vocal advocates for social reform, challenging oppressive social norms and hierarchical structures that perpetuate inequality and discrimination. Figures like Raja Ram Mohan Roy, Dayananda Saraswati, and Jyotirao Phule led movements advocating for social equality, education for all, and the abolition of discriminatory practices such as untouchability. Their tireless advocacy paved the way for transformative changes in Indian society, fostering greater inclusivity and social mobility.

2. Educational Initiatives:

Brahmins have been instrumental in promoting education as a means of empowering individuals and communities, especially those marginalized by caste-based discrimination. Through the establishment of schools, colleges, and educational institutions, Brahmin educators have provided access to knowledge and skills, enabling individuals from diverse backgrounds to pursue academic excellence and socioeconomic advancement. Their efforts have helped bridge the educational gap and promote equal opportunities for all segments of society.

3. Philanthropic Endeavors:

Brahmins have a long tradition of philanthropy and charitable giving, contributing resources and support to initiatives that address poverty, hunger, and other social ills. Through donations, endowments, and community service initiatives, Brahmins have provided relief to the needy, supported educational initiatives, and promoted healthcare access in underserved areas. Their philanthropic endeavors reflect a commitment to compassion, empathy, and social responsibility.

4. Promotion of Inter-Caste Harmony:

Brahmins have played a pivotal role in fostering inter-caste harmony and social cohesion, advocating for mutual respect, understanding, and cooperation among different caste groups. By promoting dialogue, reconciliation, and cultural exchange, Brahmins have sought to bridge divides and build inclusive communities where individuals from diverse backgrounds can coexist harmoniously. Their efforts contribute to the cultivation of a more unified and cohesive society based on shared values of equality and mutual respect.

5. Leadership in Social Movements:

Brahmins have provided leadership and guidance to social movements aimed at addressing contemporary challenges such as environmental degradation, human rights violations, and gender inequality. Figures like Swami Vivekananda and Vinoba Bhave exemplified the role of Brahmins as spiritual leaders and social reformers, inspiring individuals to work towards a more just, compassionate, and equitable society. Their visionary leadership has galvanized collective action and sparked positive change at the grassroots level.

The role of Brahmins in promoting social welfare and equality underscores their commitment to dharma, compassion, and service to humanity. Through advocacy, education, philanthropy, and inter-caste harmony initiatives, Brahmins have contributed to the advancement of social justice, empowerment, and inclusivity, leaving a lasting impact on the fabric of Indian society.

Brahmins, with their rich heritage of knowledge, spiritual wisdom, and cultural stewardship, have wielded profound influence on the development of society across the annals of Indian history. Their contributions span diverse domains, ranging from education and governance to art, literature, and social reform, shaping the cultural, intellectual, and social fabric of Indian society. Let's explore the multifaceted impact of Brahmins on societal development:

1. Preservation of Cultural Heritage:

Brahmins have played a pivotal role in preserving and transmitting India's rich cultural heritage, including its languages, literature, arts, and traditions. Through their custodianship of sacred texts, oral traditions, and ritual practices, Brahmins have safeguarded the cultural identity and spiritual legacy of Indian civilization, ensuring its continuity across generations. For example, Brahmin scholars have preserved classical music and dance forms, such as Carnatic music and Bharatanatyam, ensuring their continued relevance and vitality.

2. Promotion of Knowledge and Education:

Brahmins have been the torchbearers of knowledge and education in Indian society, fostering a culture of learning, inquiry, and intellectual pursuit. Through gurukuls (traditional schools) and vedic institutions, Brahmin scholars imparted knowledge of scriptures, philosophy, literature, and practical skills, nurturing generations of scholars, thinkers, and leaders who have contributed to the advancement of human knowledge and civilization. Figures like Adi Shankaracharya, Aryabhata, and Kalidasa have made seminal contributions to their respective fields, shaping intellectual discourse and laying the foundation for future innovations and discoveries. Their intellectual leadership has inspired generations of scholars and thinkers, fostering a culture of learning and innovation in society.

3. Governance and Leadership:

Brahmins have occupied positions of leadership and influence in governance structures, serving as advisors, administrators, and lawmakers in ancient kingdoms and empires. Endowed with wisdom, integrity, and ethical discernment, Brahmin leaders provided guidance on matters of statecraft, diplomacy, and governance, fostering stability, justice, and prosperity within their respective domains. For example, institutions like the Banaras Hindu University, founded by Pandit Madan Mohan Malaviya, have served as hubs of learning and academic excellence, empowering students to pursue their academic and professional aspirations.

4. Artistic and Literary Contributions:

Brahmins have made significant contributions to the fields of art, literature, music, and dance, enriching the cultural tapestry of India with their creative expressions and aesthetic sensibilities. From classical music maestros to renowned poets, playwrights, and artists, Brahmin luminaries have produced timeless works of beauty and inspiration that continue to resonate with audiences worldwide.

5. Social Reform and Advocacy:

Brahmins have been at the forefront of social reform movements aimed at challenging social injustices, caste-based discrimination, and oppressive social norms. Figures like Raja Ram Mohan Roy, Swami Vivekananda, and Mahatma Gandhi led movements advocating for social equality, education for all, and the empowerment of marginalized communities, catalyzing transformative changes in Indian society.

6. Spiritual and Moral Guidance:

Brahmins have provided spiritual and moral guidance to individuals and communities, nurturing a sense of ethical responsibility, compassion, and reverence for life. Through their teachings, rituals, and ethical precepts, Brahmin priests and spiritual leaders have instilled values of righteousness, non-violence, and selflessness, guiding individuals on the path of spiritual growth and moral development. Figures like Swami Vivekananda, Ramana Maharshi, and Sri Aurobindo have left a profound legacy of spiritual wisdom and moral teachings that continue to inspire millions worldwide.

The impact of Brahmins on the development of society transcends temporal and spatial boundaries, leaving an enduring legacy of cultural enrichment, intellectual enlightenment, and social transformation. By embodying the values of knowledge, service, and spiritual wisdom, Brahmins have contributed to the evolution of a more enlightened, compassionate, and harmonious society, inspiring future generations to uphold the ideals of human dignity, social justice, and collective well-being.

Chapter 10: The Brahmin and Modern Times

In the midst of rapid globalization, technological advancement, and shifting societal norms, the role of Brahmins in contemporary society stands at a critical juncture, navigating the complexities of tradition and modernity. As custodians of ancient wisdom and cultural heritage, Brahmins find themselves grappling with the imperatives of preserving tradition while embracing the demands of a dynamic and evolving world. This exploration delves into the multifaceted dimensions of the Brahmin community in modern times, shedding light on their challenges, contributions, and evolving roles in the 21st century.

In today's interconnected world, Brahmins are increasingly confronted with the pressures of globalization, technological innovation, and cultural exchange, necessitating a reevaluation of traditional practices and values in light of contemporary realities. Moreover, Brahmins are actively engaging with issues of social justice, environmental sustainability, and economic development, leveraging their intellectual leadership and cultural capital to address pressing challenges facing society. Against this backdrop, the role of Brahmins in modern times is characterized by a delicate balancing act between tradition and innovation, as they seek to adapt to the demands of a rapidly changing world while upholding the timeless principles of dharma, knowledge, and service.

As modern society undergoes rapid transformations driven by globalization, technological advancement, and socio-political shifts, Brahmins find themselves confronting a multitude of changes and challenges that reshape their roles, identities, and aspirations. Let's delve into the complexities of the modern Brahmin experience:

1. Socio-Economic Dynamics:

In contemporary society, Brahmins encounter shifting socio-economic dynamics that impact their traditional roles and livelihoods. Economic globalization, urbanization, and industrialization have disrupted traditional occupations associated with Brahmin communities, such as priesthood and agrarian pursuits. Many Brahmins are compelled to adapt to new professions, industries, and economic realities, navigating challenges of skill diversification, job market competition, and socio-economic mobility.

2. Education and Career Aspirations:

Education has traditionally been a cornerstone of Brahmin identity, with a strong emphasis on academic excellence and intellectual pursuits. However, in modern times, Brahmins face increasing pressure to excel in diverse fields beyond traditional academia, such as technology, business, and entrepreneurship. This shift in career aspirations requires Brahmins to navigate educational pathways, professional networks, and skill development initiatives to remain competitive in a rapidly evolving job market.

3. Cultural Identity and Integration:

As societies become more diverse and multicultural, Brahmins grapple with questions of cultural identity, heritage preservation, and social integration. The erosion of traditional social structures and the rise of cosmopolitanism challenge Brahmins to reconcile their cultural roots with the demands of a pluralistic society. Moreover, Brahmins face stereotypes, prejudices, and misconceptions that impact their sense of belonging and cultural pride, necessitating efforts to promote intercultural dialogue, understanding, and mutual respect.

4. Social Justice and Equity:

Brahmins are increasingly engaging with issues of social justice, equality, and inclusivity, confronting historical injustices and caste-based discrimination prevalent in Indian society. As advocates for social reform and progressive change, Brahmins advocate for policies and initiatives that address systemic inequalities, promote social mobility, and empower marginalized communities. However, Brahmins must also navigate their own privilege and historical legacies of oppression, fostering allyship and solidarity with marginalized groups in their pursuit of social justice.

5. Technological Advancement and Digital Divide:

The rapid proliferation of technology and digital connectivity presents both opportunities and challenges for Brahmins in modern society. While technological innovation facilitates access to information, education, and economic opportunities, Brahmins must contend with the digital divide, wherein disparities in access to technology and digital literacy exacerbate socio-economic inequalities. Bridging the digital divide requires concerted efforts to promote digital literacy, expand internet access, and ensure equitable participation in the digital economy.

The changes and challenges faced by Brahmins in modern society underscore the complexities of navigating tradition in a rapidly evolving world. By embracing adaptability, resilience, and innovation, Brahmins can harness the transformative potential of modernity while preserving the timeless values of their cultural heritage.

Globalization and technology have brought about significant transformations in Brahmin culture, reshaping traditional practices, values, and identities in the face of unprecedented interconnectedness and cultural exchange. While these developments offer new opportunities for cultural exchange and economic advancement, they also pose unique challenges to the preservation and adaptation of Brahmin heritage in the modern era. Let's delve into the multifaceted impact of globalization and technology on Brahmin culture:

1. Cultural Homogenization and Hybridization:

Globalization has led to the spread of Western culture and values, contributing to a homogenization of cultural practices and norms worldwide. As Brahmins interact with diverse cultures and ideologies, there is a risk of diluting or eroding traditional practices and values. Additionally, globalization has facilitated cultural hybridization, leading to the fusion of traditional Brahmin culture with global influences, creating new forms of cultural expression and identity.

2. Economic Opportunities and Challenges:

Globalization has opened up new economic opportunities for Brahmins, enabling them to participate in global markets, pursue higher education abroad, and engage in transnational business ventures. However, globalization has also led to economic disparities within Brahmin communities, exacerbating existing inequalities and widening the gap between affluent and marginalized sections. Moreover, increased competition in the global marketplace can pose challenges for traditional Brahmin professions, such as priesthood and traditional occupations.

3. Technological Advancements and Cultural Adaptation:

Technology has revolutionized communication, education, and access to information, transforming the way Brahmins engage with their cultural heritage and transmit knowledge to future generations. Digital platforms and social media have facilitated the dissemination of traditional teachings, rituals, and cultural practices, reaching a wider audience beyond geographic boundaries. However, the rapid pace of technological change also presents challenges in preserving authentic traditions and ensuring cultural continuity amidst the allure of modernization.

4. Identity and Belonging in a Globalized World:

Globalization has brought about changes in individual and collective identities, as Brahmins navigate between traditional cultural identities and globalized lifestyles. The increasing mobility of people and ideas has led to a redefinition of what it means to be a Brahmin in the modern world, with individuals grappling with questions of authenticity, assimilation, and belonging. Additionally, globalization has sparked debates within Brahmin communities about the preservation of cultural heritage, the role of tradition in contemporary life, and the tensions between modernity and tradition.

5. Preservation and Revitalization Efforts:

In response to the challenges posed by globalization and technology, Brahmins are undertaking initiatives to preserve and revitalize their cultural heritage in innovative ways. This includes efforts to document oral traditions, digitize ancient texts, and revive traditional arts and crafts. Additionally, educational institutions and cultural organizations are working to promote awareness and appreciation of Brahmin culture among younger generations, ensuring its continuity in the face of modernization pressures.

The impact of globalization and technology on Brahmin culture is multifaceted, presenting both opportunities and challenges for adaptation, preservation, and revitalization. As Brahmins navigate these changes, they must strike a delicate balance between embracing the benefits of globalization and technology while safeguarding the integrity and authenticity of their cultural heritage for future generations.

The efforts of Brahmins to adapt and preserve their traditions in the modern world

In the face of rapid globalization, technological advancement, and shifting societal dynamics, Brahmins have undertaken concerted efforts to adapt to the challenges of the modern world while preserving the richness and authenticity of their cultural traditions. These efforts reflect a commitment to honoring their heritage, fostering continuity, and ensuring the transmission of timeless values to future generations. Let's explore the multifaceted strategies employed by Brahmins to navigate the complexities of modernity while upholding their cherished traditions:

1. Embracing Technology for Cultural Preservation:

Brahmins have leveraged technological innovations to document, archive, and disseminate their cultural heritage to a global audience. Digital platforms, websites, and mobile applications have been utilized to digitize ancient texts, record oral traditions, and showcase traditional arts and rituals. By harnessing the power of technology, Brahmins are preserving their traditions in accessible and interactive formats, ensuring their relevance in the digital age.

2. Reviving Traditional Practices and Knowledge Systems:

In response to the pressures of modernization, Brahmins are actively reviving traditional practices and knowledge systems that are at risk of being lost. Initiatives such as reviving Vedic chanting, promoting classical music and dance forms, and revitalizing traditional crafts have gained momentum, fostering a renewed appreciation for the richness and diversity of Brahmin culture. Through workshops, training programs, and cultural festivals, Brahmins are passing on their ancestral knowledge to younger generations, instilling pride in their cultural heritage.

3. Promoting Education and Scholarship:

Education has always been a cornerstone of Brahmin culture, and in the modern world, Brahmins are championing educational initiatives that promote intellectual growth, critical thinking, and cultural literacy. Educational institutions, libraries, and research centers dedicated to Brahmin studies have been established, providing platforms for scholarly inquiry and interdisciplinary research. By fostering a culture of learning and intellectual curiosity, Brahmins are equipping future generations with the tools to engage with their cultural heritage in meaningful ways.

4. Advocating for Social Inclusivity and Diversity:

Recognizing the need for inclusivity and diversity in a rapidly changing world, Brahmins are actively advocating for social justice, equality, and intercultural dialogue. Efforts to challenge caste-based discrimination, promote inter-caste harmony, and engage in community outreach initiatives are gaining momentum, fostering greater cohesion and solidarity within Brahmin communities and beyond. By embracing diversity and embracing dialogue, Brahmins are fostering a more inclusive society that honors the dignity and rights of all individuals.

5. Adapting Rituals and Customs to Contemporary Contexts:

While preserving traditional rituals and customs, Brahmins are also adapting them to suit the needs and realities of contemporary life. Flexibility and innovation are key as Brahmins seek to strike a balance between honoring tradition and meeting the evolving needs of their communities.

This may involve incorporating modern elements into traditional ceremonies, adopting sustainable practices, or reinterpreting ancient teachings to address contemporary challenges such as environmental conservation and social justice.

The efforts of Brahmins to adapt and preserve their traditions in the modern world reflect a dynamic and evolving approach to cultural heritage that honors the past while embracing the future. Through innovation, education, advocacy, and cultural revitalization, Brahmins are ensuring that their cherished traditions continue to thrive and inspire future generations in an ever-changing world.

Chapter 11: Brahmins and Business

In the landscape of commerce and entrepreneurship, the role of Brahmins stands as a unique intersection of tradition, culture, and economic endeavor. Traditionally known for their scholarly pursuits, spiritual leadership, and adherence to ritualistic practices, Brahmins have also been active participants in various aspects of business and trade throughout history. However, the dynamics of Brahmins' involvement in business have evolved over time, shaped by changing socio-economic factors, cultural influences, and market demands.

This exploration delves into the

multifaceted relationship between Brahmins and business, shedding light on their historical involvement, contemporary challenges, and contributions to the entrepreneurial ecosystem. From ancient times to the modern era, Brahmins have played diverse roles in commerce, ranging from artisans and traders to professionals and entrepreneurs. As inheritors of a rich cultural heritage and entrepreneurial spirit, Brahmins continue to navigate the complexities of the marketplace while upholding their traditional values and ethical principles.

In today's globalized economy, Brahmins are actively engaged in various sectors of business, including technology, finance, hospitality, and retail, leveraging their skills, knowledge, and networks to drive innovation and economic growth. However, their involvement in business also raises questions about identity, authenticity, and the impact of modernity on traditional values. Through this exploration, we aim to uncover the nuances of Brahmins' engagement in business and the implications for their cultural identity and economic prosperity in the contemporary world.

The entrepreneurial spirit of Brahmins

Throughout history, Brahmins have demonstrated a remarkable entrepreneurial spirit, characterized by a commitment to innovation, resilience in the face of challenges, and a deep-rooted sense of ethical responsibility. This entrepreneurial ethos has manifested in various forms, from traditional artisanal pursuits to modern-day ventures in technology, finance, and beyond. Let's explore the diverse facets of the entrepreneurial spirit of Brahmins:

1. Innovation and Adaptability:

Brahmins have a long history of innovation and adaptability in their entrepreneurial endeavors. From ancient times, Brahmin artisans and craftsmen were renowned for their skill and creativity, producing exquisite works of art, textiles, and jewelry that found markets both within and outside India. In the modern era, Brahmins have embraced technological advancements and emerging industries, leveraging their intellect and creativity to pioneer new ventures and disrupt traditional markets.

2. Knowledge and Expertise:

Brahmins' pursuit of knowledge and expertise has been a driving force behind their entrepreneurial endeavors. With a strong emphasis on education and intellectual pursuits, Brahmins have acquired specialized skills and knowledge in various fields, ranging from philosophy and theology to science and finance. This deep reservoir of knowledge has enabled Brahmins to excel in diverse industries and contribute to the advancement of society through innovation and thought leadership.

3. Ethical Business Practices:

Central to the entrepreneurial spirit of Brahmins is a commitment to ethical business practices and values. Rooted in the principles of dharma (righteousness) and karma (action), Brahmins prioritize integrity, honesty, and fairness in their dealings with customers, employees, and stakeholders. This ethical foundation not only fosters trust and goodwill but also ensures the long-term sustainability and success of their ventures.

4. Community Engagement and Social Responsibility:

Brahmins have traditionally viewed entrepreneurship as a means of serving the community and promoting social welfare. Through their businesses, Brahmins have created employment opportunities, supported local artisans and craftsmen, and contributed to philanthropic initiatives that address social challenges such as poverty alleviation, education, and healthcare. This commitment to social responsibility reflects the broader ethos of service and compassion ingrained in Brahmin culture.

5. Cultural Preservation and Legacy Building:

In addition to driving economic growth and innovation, Brahmins' entrepreneurial endeavors play a crucial role in preserving and promoting their cultural heritage. Many Brahmin-owned businesses specialize in traditional arts, crafts, and cultural artifacts, serving as custodians of India's rich cultural legacy. By preserving traditional practices and supporting artisans, Brahmins ensure that their cultural heritage continues to thrive and inspire future generations.

The entrepreneurial spirit of Brahmins is characterized by a blend of innovation, expertise, ethical values, and social responsibility. Whether in traditional artisanal pursuits or modern-day startups, Brahmins continue to embody the spirit of entrepreneurship, contributing to economic prosperity, cultural preservation, and societal development in India and beyond.

Their contributions to the economy and business world

Brahmins have made significant contributions to the economy and business world, shaping industries, driving innovation, and fostering economic growth across diverse sectors. Their entrepreneurial endeavors, intellectual leadership, and ethical business practices have left an indelible mark on the economic landscape of India and beyond. Let's delve into the multifaceted contributions of Brahmins to the economy and business world:

1. Entrepreneurship and Startups:

Brahmins have been active participants in entrepreneurship and startups, founding and leading companies in various industries. From technology startups to traditional businesses, Brahmin entrepreneurs have demonstrated a penchant for innovation, risk-taking, and vision. Their ventures have not only created employment opportunities but also spurred economic development and fueled innovation ecosystems in India and abroad.

2. Intellectual Leadership and Innovation:

Brahmins have played a key role in driving intellectual leadership and innovation across sectors such as science, technology, finance, and academia. Many Brahmin professionals have made groundbreaking contributions in fields like mathematics, physics, medicine, and engineering, pioneering new discoveries, inventions, and technological advancements that have propelled economic growth and societal progress.

3. Banking and Finance:

Brahmins have a long-standing tradition of involvement in banking, finance, and commerce. Historically, Brahmin moneylenders and financiers played a crucial role in facilitating trade and commerce, providing capital to businesses, and fueling economic expansion. In the modern era, Brahmin professionals continue to excel in finance, banking, and investment management, contributing to the efficiency and stability of financial markets.

4. Education and Knowledge Economy:

Brahmins have been instrumental in the development of India's knowledge economy, with a strong emphasis on education, research, and intellectual pursuits. Many Brahmin scholars, educators, and academicians have established educational institutions, research centers, and think tanks that serve as hubs of knowledge creation and dissemination. These institutions contribute to human capital development, innovation, and economic competitiveness.

5. Cultural Industries and Tourism:

Brahmins have made significant contributions to cultural industries such as arts, literature, music, and tourism, which play a vital role in India's economy. Many Brahmin artists, writers, musicians, and performers have gained international acclaim, attracting tourists and enthusiasts from around the world. Additionally, Brahmin-owned heritage properties, temples, and cultural sites serve as major attractions for domestic and international tourists, contributing to the tourism economy.

6. Social Impact and Philanthropy:

Brahmins have a strong tradition of social impact and philanthropy, supporting charitable initiatives, community development projects, and social welfare programs. Many Brahmin-owned businesses allocate a portion of their profits towards philanthropic causes, addressing issues such as education, healthcare, poverty alleviation, and environmental conservation. This commitment to social responsibility contributes to inclusive growth and sustainable development.

The contributions of Brahmins to the economy and business world encompass a wide range of activities, from entrepreneurship and innovation to intellectual leadership, finance, education, and social impact. Their collective efforts have not only driven economic growth and prosperity but also enriched India's cultural heritage, promoted social welfare, and advanced the common good.

Chapter 12: Brahmins and Art

In the vibrant tapestry of Indian culture, the role of Brahmins in fostering artistic expression and creativity stands as a testament to their rich heritage and cultural legacy. From ancient times to the modern era, Brahmins have played a pivotal role in shaping various art forms, including music, dance, literature, painting, sculpture, and architecture. This exploration delves into the multifaceted relationship between Brahmins and art, shedding light on their historical contributions, contemporary endeavors, and enduring influence on India's artistic landscape.

Throughout history, Brahmins have been

patrons, practitioners, and preservers of art, serving as custodians of artistic traditions and repositories of cultural knowledge. Their deep spiritual beliefs, philosophical insights, and reverence for aesthetics have found expression in diverse art forms, reflecting the ethos of dharma (righteousness), bhakti (devotion), and samskara (cultural refinement). From the sacred chants of the Vedas to the intricate sculptures of temple architecture, Brahmins have imbued Indian art with spiritual significance, symbolic meaning, and timeless beauty.

In today's rapidly evolving world, Brahmins continue to uphold their artistic heritage while embracing contemporary trends and innovations. Through their creative endeavors, they not only preserve ancient traditions but also contribute to the dynamic cultural milieu of modern India.

From classical musicians and dancers to contemporary artists and filmmakers, Brahmins play a vital role in shaping India's artistic identity, fostering cross-cultural dialogue, and inspiring future generations to celebrate the richness and diversity of Indian art.

The role of Brahmins in promoting and preserving Indian art forms

Brahmins have played a pivotal role in promoting and preserving Indian art forms, serving as custodians of cultural heritage and guardians of artistic traditions. Their contributions span various disciplines, including music, dance, literature, painting, sculpture, and architecture, enriching India's artistic legacy and shaping its cultural identity. Let's delve into the multifaceted ways in which Brahmins have championed Indian art forms:

1. Preservation of Traditional Knowledge:

Brahmins have preserved and transmitted traditional knowledge systems related to Indian art forms through oral traditions, scriptures, and guru-shishya parampara (teacher-disciple lineage). For centuries, Brahmin gurus (teachers) have imparted sacred chants (mantras), musical compositions (ragas), dance forms (mudras), and literary works (kavyas) to their disciples, ensuring the continuity of artistic traditions across generations.

2. Promotion of Classical Music and Dance:

Brahmins have been instrumental in promoting classical music (such as Hindustani and Carnatic) and dance forms (such as Bharatanatyam, Kathak, Odissi, and

Kuchipudi) through performance, education, and patronage. Many renowned musicians, composers, and dancers hail from Brahmin families and have contributed significantly to the development and popularization of Indian classical arts both nationally and internationally.

3. Patronage of Temple Architecture and Sculpture:

Brahmins have been patrons of temple architecture and sculpture, commissioning and funding the construction of magnificent temples adorned with intricate carvings and sculptures depicting Hindu deities, mythological narratives, and spiritual symbolism. These architectural marvels, such as the temples of Khajuraho, Konark, and Hampi, stand as testaments to Brahmins' contributions to India's architectural heritage.

4. Literary Contributions and Philanthropy:

Brahmins have made significant literary contributions to Indian literature, producing epics, scriptures, poetry, and philosophical treatises that reflect the ethos of Indian culture and spirituality. Additionally, Brahmin philanthropists have supported the publication of literary works, the establishment of libraries and educational institutions, and the preservation of ancient manuscripts, fostering a culture of literary excellence and intellectual inquiry.

5. Transmission of Artistic Values and Aesthetics:

Brahmins have transmitted artistic values, aesthetics, and ethical principles inherent in Indian art forms, emphasizing the importance of bhakti (devotion), rasa (emotional resonance), and samskara (cultural refinement). Through their teachings, performances, and artistic endeavors, Brahmins have instilled a sense of cultural pride and spiritual resonance in Indian art, fostering a deeper appreciation for its beauty and significance.

The role of Brahmins in promoting and preserving Indian art forms is multifaceted, encompassing aspects of education, performance, patronage, and cultural transmission. Their enduring contributions have enriched India's artistic heritage, inspired generations of artists and enthusiasts, and reinforced the cultural fabric of the nation.

Chapter 13: The Brahmin Women

In the intricate tapestry of Brahmin society, the role of women stands as a dynamic and evolving facet, blending tradition with the winds of change. Brahmin women have long been the custodians of cultural heritage, guardians of familial values, and contributors to the socio-economic fabric of society. This exploration delves into the multifaceted lives of Brahmin women, spanning traditional roles, evolving aspirations, and the quest for empowerment amidst shifting paradigms.

Traditionally, Brahmin women have played pivotal roles in upholding familial traditions, preserving cultural rituals, and nurturing future generations with values steeped in dharma (righteousness) and samskara (cultural refinement). From managing household affairs to participating in religious ceremonies and community activities, Brahmin women have been the pillars of support within their families and communities.

However, as society progresses and embraces modernity, Brahmin women are also navigating new avenues of education, career pursuits, and self-expression. With increasing access to education and opportunities, many Brahmin women are charting their paths in diverse fields such as academia, entrepreneurship, arts, and social activism, challenging traditional gender norms and redefining societal expectations.

In Brahmin society, women play multifaceted roles that encompass traditional duties, familial responsibilities, and increasingly, participation in various spheres of public life. These roles are shaped by cultural norms, religious beliefs, and societal expectations, reflecting a delicate balance between tradition and evolving aspirations. Let's delve into the intricacies of the role of women in Brahmin society:

1. Guardians of Tradition:

Brahmin women are often regarded as the custodians of tradition, responsible for upholding cultural rituals, religious ceremonies, and familial customs. They play a central role in transmitting cultural knowledge, passing down ancestral practices, and preserving the rich heritage of Brahmin culture for future generations.

2. Family and Household Management:

Brahmin women traditionally assume the primary responsibility for managing household affairs, including cooking, cleaning, and caregiving. They play a pivotal role in maintaining domestic harmony, nurturing family relationships, and ensuring the well-being of household members through their care and dedication.

3. Education and Cultural Transmission:

Brahmin women are instrumental in the education and cultural transmission of children within the family. They impart moral values, religious teachings, and cultural traditions to the younger generation, instilling a sense of identity, pride, and belonging in Brahmin heritage.

4. Spiritual and Religious Practices:

Brahmin women actively participate in spiritual and religious practices, often taking on roles in religious ceremonies, rituals, and festivals. They contribute to the performance of pujas (ritual worship), recitation of sacred texts, and observance of religious rites, fostering a sense of spirituality and devotion within the family and community.

5. Supportive Roles in Public Life:

While Brahmin women have historically been confined to domestic spheres, there is a growing trend of their participation in various aspects of public life. Many Brahmin women are pursuing education, careers, and leadership roles in fields such as academia, business, politics, and social activism, challenging traditional gender roles and contributing to societal progress.

6. Agents of Change and Empowerment:

In recent years, Brahmin women have increasingly asserted their agency and pursued avenues for empowerment and self-expression. They are advocating for gender equality, women's rights, and social justice, driving positive change within Brahmin society and beyond.

The role of women in Brahmin society is characterized by a nuanced interplay of tradition, empowerment, and evolution. While they continue to uphold traditional values and familial responsibilities, Brahmin women are also embracing opportunities for education, career advancement, and societal engagement, enriching the fabric of Brahmin culture and contributing to the broader discourse on gender equality and empowerment.

The challenges faced by Brahmin women in traditional roles and expectations

While Brahmin women have long been respected for their contributions to family and community, they also encounter unique challenges stemming from traditional roles and societal expectations. These challenges, rooted in cultural norms and gender dynamics, can constrain their autonomy, limit their opportunities, and impede their personal and professional growth. Let's explore some of the key challenges faced by Brahmin women in traditional roles:

1. Gender-Based Expectations:

Brahmin society often imposes rigid gender roles, prescribing specific behaviors, duties, and responsibilities for women based on traditional norms. These expectations may prioritize domestic duties over personal aspirations, restrict opportunities for education and career advancement, and reinforce stereotypes about women's roles as caregivers and homemakers.

2. Limited Educational Opportunities:

Historically, Brahmin women have faced barriers to accessing formal education and pursuing higher learning opportunities. Cultural expectations may prioritize their roles within the household, leading to limited support for their educational pursuits and career aspirations. This lack of access to education can hinder their intellectual development, economic independence, and social mobility.

3. Social Stigma and Pressure:

Brahmin women may face social stigma and scrutiny if they deviate from traditional norms or challenge gendered expectations. Pressure to conform to societal ideals of femininity, modesty, and obedience can create a sense of constraint and suppression, inhibiting their ability to express themselves freely and pursue their interests and passions.

4. Marital Expectations and Arranged Marriages:

Brahmin women often encounter pressure to adhere to marital expectations, including early marriage, arranged unions, and adherence to caste and community preferences. These expectations may limit their autonomy in choosing life partners, negotiating marital terms, and pursuing relationships based on mutual consent and compatibility.

5. Balancing Family and Career:

Brahmin women face the challenge of balancing their familial responsibilities with career aspirations and professional pursuits. Traditional expectations may prioritize their roles as wives and mothers, leading to limited opportunities for career advancement, work-life balance, and personal fulfillment outside the domestic sphere.

6. Limited Representation in Leadership Roles:

Despite their intellectual capabilities and contributions to family and community, Brahmin women are often underrepresented in leadership roles within both traditional and modern contexts. Cultural biases and patriarchal norms may hinder their access to positions of authority, decision-making power, and influence, perpetuating gender disparities and inequalities.

Brahmin women grapple with a myriad of challenges arising from traditional roles and expectations, which can impact their personal growth, autonomy, and well-being. Addressing these challenges requires collective efforts to challenge gender norms, promote equal opportunities, and create supportive environments that empower Brahmin women to fulfill their potential and contribute meaningfully to society.

The changing roles and empowerment of Brahmin women in modern times

In contemporary society, Brahmin women are experiencing a transformation in their roles and opportunities, marked by greater access to education, economic independence, and participation in various spheres of public life. This shift reflects evolving attitudes towards gender equality, individual autonomy, and women's empowerment. Let's delve into the changing roles and empowerment of Brahmin women in modern times:

1. Education and Career Opportunities:

One of the most significant changes for Brahmin women in modern times is the increased access to education and career opportunities. Many Brahmin women are pursuing higher education, professional degrees, and vocational training, enabling them to enter diverse fields such as medicine, law, engineering, academia, business, and the arts. This educational empowerment equips them with the knowledge, skills, and confidence to pursue their aspirations and contribute meaningfully to society.

2. Economic Independence:

With education and career advancement, Brahmin women are achieving greater economic independence and financial stability. They are entering the workforce, starting businesses, and engaging in entrepreneurial ventures, thereby contributing to household incomes, supporting their families, and making independent financial decisions. This economic empowerment enhances their agency, autonomy, and socio-economic status within their communities.

3. Leadership and Representation:

Brahmin women are increasingly assuming leadership roles and positions of influence in various sectors, including politics, governance, academia, media, and civil society. They are breaking barriers, shattering stereotypes, and challenging traditional gender norms by occupying positions of authority, decision-making, and advocacy. Their representation in leadership roles brings diverse perspectives, innovative ideas, and inclusive governance practices, contributing to positive social change and women's empowerment.

4. Advocacy for Gender Equality:

Brahmin women are actively engaged in advocacy efforts to promote gender equality, women's rights, and social justice. They are raising awareness about gender-based discrimination, violence against women, and systemic barriers to women's empowerment. Through grassroots movements, community organizing, and activism, Brahmin women are amplifying their voices, demanding policy reforms, and driving collective action to advance gender equality agendas.

5. Redefining Gender Roles and Relationships:

In modern times, Brahmin women are redefining traditional gender roles and relationships within their families and communities. They are challenging stereotypes about women's roles as solely caregivers and homemakers, advocating for shared responsibilities, mutual respect, and egalitarian partnerships. This shift towards more equitable gender dynamics fosters healthier family dynamics, promotes work-life balance, and cultivates supportive environments for women's personal and professional growth.

The changing roles and empowerment of Brahmin women in modern times signify a progressive shift towards greater gender equality, individual agency, and social inclusion. As they continue to navigate evolving opportunities and challenges, Brahmin women are reshaping narratives, breaking barriers, and contributing to a more inclusive and equitable society for future generations.

Chapter 14: The Brahmin and Inter-caste Marriages

Inter-caste marriages have long been a subject of societal scrutiny and cultural discourse in India, reflecting the intersection of tradition, identity, and social dynamics. Among the diverse communities in India, Brahmins, as custodians of cultural heritage and guardians of tradition, grapple with unique considerations and complexities when it comes to inter-caste unions.

In ancient times, as mentioned earlier, there were no rigid caste distinctions, and a person's character and virtues were considered paramount. However, with the distortion in society, the rigid caste system emerged, delineating societal hierarchies and perpetuating social divisions. Nevertheless, in the contemporary era marked by globalization and cultural exchange, these boundaries are gradually dissolving. Brahmins, recognizing the evolving social landscape, are increasingly embracing inter-caste marriages, transcending traditional caste barriers and fostering inclusivity within their communities.

Inter-caste marriages among Brahmins challenge traditional notions of caste purity, lineage, and social hierarchy, often prompting introspection and negotiation of cultural values and familial expectations. These unions transcend caste barriers, fostering cross-cultural exchanges, and reshaping perceptions of identity and belonging within Brahmin communities. Moreover, they signify a progressive shift towards a more inclusive and egalitarian society, where individuals are valued for their character and merit rather than their caste background.

The history and prevalence of inter-caste marriages among Brahmins

Inter-caste marriages among Brahmins have a nuanced history shaped by cultural, social, and historical factors. While the concept of inter-caste marriages may seem relatively modern, historical evidence suggests that such unions have occurred sporadically throughout ancient and medieval India. However, their prevalence and acceptance varied depending on regional customs, religious beliefs, and societal norms.

1. Ancient Times:

In ancient Indian society, including the Vedic period, inter-caste marriages were not unheard of, and societal divisions were not as rigid as they later became. Marriage alliances were often based on factors such as mutual consent, compatibility, and familial considerations rather than rigid adherence to caste boundaries. Brahmins, as learned individuals respected for their knowledge and wisdom, sometimes formed marital unions with individuals from other varnas based on shared values and common interests.

2. Medieval Period:

During the medieval period, especially under various dynasties and kingdoms, inter-caste marriages among Brahmins continued to occur, albeit with more emphasis on preserving caste purity and lineage. While Brahmins held a position of prestige and authority in society, marriage alliances were often used strategically to forge political alliances, consolidate power, or secure economic advantages.

3. Colonial Era:

The colonial era witnessed significant transformations in Indian society, including the introduction of new laws and social reforms. With the advent of British colonial rule, inter-caste marriages faced increasing scrutiny and regulation, as the colonial administration sought to codify and standardize social practices. However, despite these changes, inter-caste marriages persisted, albeit often clandestinely, as individuals sought to navigate societal expectations and personal desires.

4. Modern Times:

In contemporary times, inter-caste marriages among Brahmins have become more visible and socially acceptable, reflecting shifting attitudes towards caste, marriage, and individual autonomy. Factors such as urbanization, education, economic independence, and exposure to diverse cultures have contributed to the increasing prevalence of inter-caste marriages among Brahmins. Moreover, globalization has facilitated greater intermingling and interaction between people from different castes, fostering a more inclusive and pluralistic society.

5. Prevalence and Acceptance:

While inter-caste marriages among Brahmins were historically less common due to societal norms and caste restrictions, their prevalence has been gradually increasing in recent decades. Many Brahmins are now open to marrying individuals from other castes, prioritizing factors such as compatibility, shared values, and personal happiness over caste considerations. However, acceptance of inter-caste marriages still varies among different Brahmin communities and is influenced by factors such as regional customs, family traditions, and individual beliefs.

The history and prevalence of inter-caste marriages among Brahmins reflect the dynamic nature of Indian society, where tradition intersects with modernity, and cultural norms evolve over time. While inter-caste marriages were historically less common due to societal constraints, changing attitudes and societal dynamics have contributed to their increasing acceptance and prevalence among

Brahmins in contemporary times.

The challenges and controversies surrounding inter-caste marriages

Inter-caste marriages, while increasingly accepted in modern times, continue to face challenges and controversies rooted in deep-seated societal norms, cultural traditions, and historical prejudices. These challenges often manifest in various forms and impact individuals, families, and communities involved in such unions. Let's explore some of the key challenges and controversies surrounding inter-caste marriages:

1. Social Stigma and Discrimination:

Inter-caste marriages are often met with

social stigma and discrimination, particularly in communities where caste identities are deeply entrenched. Families may face ostracism, ridicule, or social exclusion, while couples may encounter prejudice, judgment, and even hostility from relatives, neighbors, and community members. This social stigma can lead to psychological distress, emotional trauma, and strained relationships within families and communities.

2. Family Opposition and Conflict:

One of the most significant challenges faced by couples in inter-caste marriages is opposition and conflict from their families. Traditional families may resist such unions due to concerns about caste purity, social status, and familial honor. This opposition can result in familial estrangement, disapproval, or even disinheritance, creating significant emotional and financial hardships for the couples involved.

3. Legal and Administrative Hurdles:

Inter-caste marriages may encounter legal and administrative hurdles, particularly in regions where caste-based laws or regulations exist. Couples may face bureaucratic obstacles, delays, or even legal challenges when registering their marriages or securing official documentation. These hurdles can exacerbate the stress and uncertainty already present in inter-caste marriages, complicating matters further for the couples involved.

4. Cultural Clashes and Adjustments:

Inter-caste marriages often entail navigating cultural differences, traditions, and rituals associated with each partner's caste background. Couples may face challenges in reconciling contrasting customs, religious practices, and family traditions, leading to conflicts or misunderstandings. Moreover, societal expectations and pressures to conform to specific cultural norms can strain the relationship and hinder mutual understanding and acceptance.

5. Economic and Social Disparities:

Inter-caste marriages may also highlight existing economic and social disparities between partners from different castes. Disparities in educational attainment, economic status, and social privileges can create power imbalances within the relationship and contribute to feelings of insecurity or resentment. Addressing these disparities and fostering equitable partnerships requires open communication, mutual respect, and shared decision-making.

6. Community Backlash and Resistance:

In some cases, inter-caste marriages may provoke backlash and resistance from conservative or orthodox community members who view such unions as a threat to traditional values or caste purity. Couples may face opposition, protests, or even violence from extremist groups or caste-based organizations seeking to maintain societal hierarchies and preserve caste identities. This resistance can further exacerbate tensions and create a hostile environment for inter-caste couples.

The challenges and controversies surrounding inter-caste marriages underscore the deep-rooted social divisions, cultural prejudices, and systemic inequalities prevalent in many societies. Overcoming these challenges requires concerted efforts to promote tolerance, acceptance, and equality, while challenging discriminatory attitudes and practices that perpetuate caste-based discrimination and social exclusion. Through dialogue, education, and advocacy, we can strive towards building a more inclusive and equitable society where individuals are free to love and marry irrespective of caste, creed, or social status.

The changing attitudes towards inter-caste marriages in Brahmin society

In Brahmin society, attitudes towards inter-caste marriages have undergone significant transformation over the years, reflecting evolving societal norms, cultural shifts, and individual aspirations. While traditionally frowned upon due to concerns about caste purity and social status, there is a discernible shift towards greater acceptance and openness towards inter-caste unions among many Brahmins. Let's delve into the changing attitudes towards inter-caste marriages in Brahmin society:

1. Shift from Caste-based to Compatibility-based Matchmaking:

Traditionally, marriages in Brahmin society were primarily arranged within the same caste, emphasizing the importance of preserving caste purity and lineage. However, there is a growing recognition that compatibility, shared values, and personal compatibility are more crucial factors for marital success than caste identity alone. Many Brahmin families are now prioritizing these factors over caste considerations when seeking potential matches for their children, leading to a more inclusive approach to matchmaking.

2. Emphasis on Individual Autonomy and Choice:

With increasing exposure to modern education, urbanization, and globalization, Brahmin youth are asserting their autonomy and agency in matters of love and marriage. They are challenging traditional parental authority and societal expectations, advocating for the right to choose their life partners based on personal preferences, rather than caste compatibility. This shift reflects a broader trend towards individualism and self-determination in contemporary Brahmin society.

3. Influence of Education and Exposure:

Education plays a pivotal role in shaping attitudes towards inter-caste marriages among Brahmins. Educated Brahmins, particularly those who have been exposed to diverse cultures, ideas, and perspectives, tend to be more open-minded and receptive to inter-caste unions. They recognize the arbitrary nature of caste distinctions and prioritize qualities such as education, character, and compatibility in their marital choices, irrespective of caste boundaries.

4. Impact of Social Movements and Advocacy:

Social movements and advocacy efforts promoting social justice, equality, and human rights have also influenced attitudes towards inter-caste marriages in Brahmin society. These movements have challenged caste-based discrimination and stigma, fostering a more inclusive and egalitarian ethos that values diversity and celebrates individual choices. As a result, many Brahmins are embracing inter-caste marriages as a means of challenging casteism and promoting social harmony.

5. Changing Demographics and Urbanization:

The demographic shifts and urbanization processes occurring in Brahmin communities have also contributed to changing attitudes towards inter-caste marriages. Urban areas, characterized by greater diversity, cosmopolitanism, and exposure to alternative lifestyles, tend to be more accepting of inter-caste unions compared to rural areas. As more Brahmins migrate to urban centers and engage with diverse social networks, they are increasingly exposed to alternative perspectives and lifestyles, which can influence their attitudes towards inter-caste marriages.

The changing attitudes towards inter-caste marriages in Brahmin society reflect broader shifts towards individualism, egalitarianism, and inclusivity. While traditional norms and cultural values continue to influence marital preferences to some extent, there is a noticeable trend towards greater acceptance and openness towards inter-caste unions among many Brahmins, driven by factors such as education, exposure, and advocacy for social justice. As Brahmin society continues to evolve, it is likely that attitudes towards inter-caste marriages will continue to evolve as well, reflecting the changing dynamics of contemporary Indian society.

Chapter 15: The Brahmin and Reservation

In the intricate tapestry of India's social fabric, the topic of reservation has emerged as a contentious issue, stirring debates, controversies, and societal divisions. At the heart of this discourse lies the question of social justice, equity, and representation for marginalized communities. Among the various groups affected by reservation policies, the Brahmins, as a community historically associated with privilege and influence, find themselves navigating a complex landscape of entitlement, disadvantage, and identity politics.

Reservation, as a policy measure aimed at addressing historical injustices and systemic inequalities, has been a cornerstone of India's affirmative action initiatives since independence. However, its implementation and impact have sparked intense debates and controversies, particularly regarding its efficacy, fairness, and unintended consequences. Brahmins, as a community historically perceived to have held positions of privilege and dominance, have found themselves at the center of these debates, grappling with questions of representation, meritocracy, and social equity.

Reservation, as a policy measure aimed at promoting social justice and equity, has had a profound impact on Indian society, affecting various communities, including Brahmins. The concept of reservation, introduced as affirmative action to address historical injustices and systemic inequalities, has sparked intense debates and controversies, particularly among Brahmins who perceive themselves as affected by its implementation. Let's delve into the concept of reservation and its impact on Brahmins:

1. Historical Context:

Reservation policies were introduced in India following independence to uplift marginalized communities such as Scheduled Castes (SC), Scheduled Tribes (ST), and Other Backward Classes (OBCs), who historically faced discrimination and exclusion. These policies aimed to provide opportunities for education, employment, and political representation to those who were historically disadvantaged due to caste-based discrimination and social inequality.

2. Perceived Disadvantages for Brahmins:

Brahmins, traditionally perceived as a privileged group in Indian society, have expressed concerns about the impact of reservation on their access to education, employment, and other opportunities. Some Brahmins argue that reservation policies have led to a perceived "reverse discrimination," where they feel marginalized or excluded from certain opportunities due to quotas reserved for other caste groups.

3. Challenges in Education and Employment:

Brahmins, who historically held positions of influence in academia, government, and other sectors, have faced challenges in accessing educational institutions and employment opportunities due to reservation policies. Many Brahmin students and professionals feel that they have to compete against candidates from reserved categories who may have lower academic qualifications but benefit from reservation quotas.

4. Economic Implications:

Reservation policies have also raised economic concerns among Brahmins, particularly those from economically disadvantaged backgrounds. Brahmins who do not benefit from reservation quotas may face economic hardships due to increased competition for limited resources and opportunities in a society where caste-based preferences still play a significant role.

5. Social Identity and Stigma:

Reservation policies have also impacted the social identity and stigma associated with being a Brahmin. Some Brahmins feel stigmatized or marginalized due to stereotypes and misconceptions about their community's socio-economic status and privileges, perpetuated by the discourse surrounding reservation.

6. Calls for Reform and Meritocracy:

Many Brahmins advocate for reforms in reservation policies, emphasizing the need for a more merit-based approach to education and employment. They argue that reservation should be based on socio-economic criteria rather than caste alone, ensuring that individuals from all backgrounds have equal opportunities to succeed based on their abilities and qualifications.

The concept of reservation has had a multifaceted impact on Brahmins, affecting their access to education, employment, and social opportunities, while also shaping perceptions of identity, privilege, and social justice within the community. While reservation policies aim to address historical injustices and promote inclusivity, their implementation has raised complex challenges and debates among Brahmins and other stakeholders in Indian society. Efforts to strike a balance between affirmative action and meritocracy remain ongoing, reflecting the ongoing struggle for social equality and justice in a diverse and complex society.

The debates and controversies surrounding reservation for Brahmins

Reservation for Brahmins, a topic steeped in complexity and contention, has been a subject of intense debate and controversy within Indian society. While reservation policies were initially introduced to address historical injustices and social inequalities faced by marginalized communities, the inclusion of Brahmins within the ambit of reservation has sparked heated discussions, raising questions about fairness, representation, and social justice. Let's delve into the debates and controversies surrounding reservation for Brahmins:

1. Perceptions of Privilege and Disadvantage:

One of the central themes in the debate surrounding reservation for Brahmins is the perception of their historical privilege juxtaposed with their perceived disadvantage under reservation policies. While Brahmins have traditionally held positions of influence and authority in society, some argue that they also face socio-economic challenges and barriers, particularly among those from economically disadvantaged backgrounds.

2. Reverse Discrimination vs. Social Justice:

A key point of contention revolves around the concept of "reverse discrimination," where Brahmins argue that they face discrimination and exclusion due to reservation policies favoring other caste groups. Conversely, proponents of reservation for Brahmins argue that it is necessary to address the socio-economic disparities and systemic inequalities faced by certain segments of the Brahmin community.

3. Meritocracy vs. Affirmative Action:

The debate also touches upon the principles of meritocracy versus affirmative action. Critics of reservation for Brahmins often argue that merit should be the sole criterion for educational and employment opportunities, regardless of caste or social background. On the other hand, advocates for reservation argue that affirmative action is essential to level the playing field and provide equal opportunities for historically marginalized communities, including Brahmins from disadvantaged backgrounds.

4. Socio-economic Criteria vs. Caste-based Reservation:

Another point of contention is the criteria used for reservation. While some advocate for reservation based solely on socio-economic factors, others argue for caste-based reservation to address historical injustices and systemic discrimination. The inclusion of Brahmins within reservation policies further complicates this debate, as it challenges traditional notions of caste privilege and disadvantage.

5. Regional Variations and Political Dynamics:

Debates surrounding reservation for Brahmins also vary regionally, reflecting the diverse socio-political landscapes and caste dynamics across different states and communities in India. Political parties often exploit these regional variations to garner support or mobilize opposition, further complicating the discourse on reservation for Brahmins.

6. Calls for Reforms and Alternative Solutions:

Amidst the debates and controversies, there are calls for reforms and alternative solutions to address socio-economic disparities and ensure equitable access to opportunities for all. Some advocate for targeted welfare programs, skill development initiatives, and education reforms as alternatives to caste-based reservation, while others propose revisions to reservation policies to make them more inclusive and effective.

The debates and controversies surrounding reservation for Brahmins underscore the complex interplay of historical, socio-economic, and political factors shaping India's affirmative action policies. While reservation aims to address historical injustices and promote social justice, its implementation and impact on Brahmins raise complex ethical, legal, and societal questions that continue to fuel heated discussions and debates within Indian society. Efforts to find common ground and achieve consensus on this contentious issue remain ongoing, reflecting the broader struggle for equality and justice in a diverse and dynamic democracy like India.

As the discourse surrounding reservation
policies continues to evolve in India, the
inclusion of Brahmins within the reservation
framework has become a subject of
considerable scrutiny and debate. The
current state of reservation for Brahmins
and its implications reflect the intricate
interplay of socio-political dynamics,
historical contexts, and contemporary
challenges. Let's delve into the details:

1. Limited Reservation Provisions:

Currently, reservation provisions for
Brahmins are limited and vary across states
and regions in India. While some states
have implemented reservation quotas for
economically backward sections among

Brahmins, others do not have specific reservation policies targeting the Brahmin community. This variation underscores the decentralized nature of reservation policies and the complexities involved in addressing the diverse socio-economic realities of different communities.

2. Legal Challenges and Court Interventions:

The implementation of reservation policies for Brahmins has also faced legal challenges and court interventions. Brahmin organizations and individuals have filed petitions questioning the constitutionality and fairness of reservation provisions, leading to judicial scrutiny and rulings on the matter. Court decisions regarding reservation for Brahmins have varied, with some upholding existing policies while others advocating for reforms or modifications.

3. Socio-political Backlash and Opposition:

The prospect of reservation for Brahmins has generated socio-political backlash and opposition from various quarters. Some political parties and social groups argue against extending reservation benefits to Brahmins, citing concerns about caste-based politics, resource allocation, and the dilution of existing reservation quotas for historically marginalized communities. This opposition reflects broader debates about identity politics, social justice, and representation in Indian society.

4. Socio-economic Realities and Challenges:

The current state of reservation for Brahmins also intersects with their socio-economic realities and challenges. While Brahmins have historically been associated with positions of privilege and influence, there are segments within the community that face socio-economic hardships and disparities. Reservation policies targeting economically backward sections among Brahmins aim to address these disparities and provide opportunities for upward mobility and social inclusion.

5. Implications for Social Cohesion and Equity:

The implications of reservation for Brahmins extend beyond legal and political considerations to broader questions of social cohesion and equity. Proponents argue that reservation can help address socio-economic disparities and promote inclusivity within the community, fostering a more equitable society. Critics, however, raise concerns about the potential polarizing effects of caste-based reservation and its impact on inter-community relations.

6. Need for Dialogue and Reconciliation:

Given the complex nature of reservation policies and their implications for Brahmins and Indian society at large, there is a pressing need for dialogue, reconciliation, and consensus-building. Engaging in constructive discussions, acknowledging diverse perspectives, and finding common ground are essential for addressing the challenges posed by reservation and advancing towards a more just and inclusive society.

The current state of reservation for Brahmins reflects the intricate web of socio-political dynamics, legal complexities, and socio-economic realities shaping India's affirmative action policies. While reservation aims to address historical injustices and promote social equity, its implementation and implications for Brahmins highlight the ongoing challenges and debates surrounding caste, identity, and social justice in contemporary India. Finding sustainable solutions that balance the needs of different communities and uphold constitutional principles of equality and justice remains a paramount task for policymakers, activists, and society at large.

Chapter 16: The Brahmin and Social Justice

The intersection of Brahmin identity with the broader concept of social justice in India is a topic steeped in complexity, historical context, and contemporary relevance. Brahmins, as a community traditionally associated with knowledge, spirituality, and social influence, occupy a unique position within the intricate tapestry of India's social fabric. The discourse surrounding the role of Brahmins in promoting social justice encompasses a spectrum of perspectives, ranging from historical narratives to present-day realities. This introduction aims to explore the multifaceted dimensions of the Brahmin community's engagement with social justice, examining their responsibilities, challenges, and contributions in fostering a more equitable society.

The role of Brahmins in promoting social justice and equality

As custodians of knowledge and guardians of tradition, Brahmins have historically played pivotal roles in shaping India's cultural, spiritual, and intellectual landscape. Their influence extends across domains such as education, religion, politics, and social welfare, imbuing them with a profound sense of responsibility towards societal well-being. However, this privileged position also brings with it inherent tensions, as Brahmins grapple with issues of privilege, identity, and social accountability in an increasingly diverse and dynamic society.

The Brahmin community, historically regarded as custodians of knowledge and spiritual wisdom in Indian society, has played a multifaceted role in promoting social justice and equality. This role encompasses various dimensions, ranging from religious and educational activities to advocacy for societal reforms.

1. Education and Knowledge Dissemination:

Brahmins have traditionally been associated with education and intellectual pursuits, serving as educators, scholars, and custodians of sacred texts. By imparting knowledge and facilitating intellectual discourse, Brahmins have played a pivotal role in empowering individuals from all sections of society, thereby contributing to the promotion of social equality through education.

2. Advocacy for Social Reforms:

Throughout history, Brahmins have been instrumental in advocating for social reforms aimed at challenging discriminatory practices and promoting social equality. Leaders and thinkers from the Brahmin community have actively participated in movements against caste-based discrimination, untouchability, and other social injustices, advocating for a more inclusive and equitable society.

3. Religious and Spiritual Leadership:

As leaders in religious and spiritual domains, Brahmins have leveraged their influence to promote ethical values, compassion, and social responsibility. Through religious discourses, rituals, and community initiatives, Brahmins have advocated for principles of social justice, emphasizing the importance of compassion, empathy, and service to humanity.

4. Participation in Social Welfare Activities:

Brahmins have been actively involved in various social welfare activities aimed at uplifting marginalized communities and addressing socio-economic disparities. From running educational institutions and healthcare facilities to providing humanitarian aid and support, Brahmins have contributed to grassroots initiatives that promote social justice and empowerment.

5. Mentorship and Guidance:

Brahmins have served as mentors and guides to individuals from diverse backgrounds, offering guidance, support, and mentorship in personal, academic, and professional spheres. By fostering relationships based on mutual respect and collaboration, Brahmins have facilitated social mobility and empowerment, thereby contributing to greater social equality.

6. Intellectual Leadership and Advocacy:

Brahmins have often assumed leadership roles in intellectual, cultural, and political spheres, advocating for policies and initiatives that promote social justice and equality. Through intellectual discourse, critical inquiry, and advocacy, Brahmins have challenged societal norms and structures that perpetuate inequality, advocating for systemic reforms and inclusive policies.

The role of Brahmins in promoting social justice and equality is multifaceted and dynamic, encompassing educational, religious, advocacy, and community engagement initiatives. As torchbearers of knowledge and guardians of tradition, Brahmins have played a significant role in shaping India's social conscience and fostering a more just and equitable society. However, challenges remain, and ongoing efforts are needed to address systemic inequalities and promote social justice for all members of society.

While Brahmins have endeavored to promote social justice and inclusivity, their efforts have been met with various challenges and criticisms. These hurdles stem from historical legacies, societal perceptions, and contemporary complexities, posing significant obstacles to their pursuit of social justice. Let's explore in detail the challenges and criticisms faced by Brahmins in this endeavor:

1. Historical Privilege and Perceptions:

Brahmins have historically occupied privileged positions in society, serving as custodians of knowledge and enjoying socio-economic advantages. As a result, their involvement in social justice initiatives is sometimes met with skepticism and accusations of hypocrisy. Critics argue that Brahmins, as beneficiaries of the caste system, are inherently complicit in perpetuating social inequalities, thereby undermining their credibility in advocating for social justice.

2. Stereotypes and Prejudices:

Brahmins often face stereotypes and prejudices that overshadow their contributions to social justice. They are sometimes portrayed as elitist, conservative, or disconnected from the realities of marginalized communities, leading to marginalization and mistrust within broader social justice movements. These stereotypes not only undermine the legitimacy of Brahmin-led initiatives but also hinder meaningful dialogue and collaboration across caste lines.

3. Resistance from Traditionalists:

Traditionalist elements within the Brahmin community may resist efforts to challenge caste-based hierarchies and advocate for social justice. They may view such initiatives as a threat to traditional norms and cultural practices, leading to internal divisions and conflicts within the community. Resistance from traditionalists can impede progress towards greater inclusivity and social equality, perpetuating existing power dynamics and inequalities.

4. Backlash from Conservative Groups:

Brahmins advocating for social justice may face backlash from conservative groups and caste-based organizations that seek to maintain the status quo. These groups may perceive Brahmin involvement in social justice initiatives as a challenge to their own vested interests and caste-based privileges, leading to hostility and opposition. The fear of reprisal or social ostracism can deter Brahmins from actively engaging in social justice advocacy.

5. Political Instrumentalization:

Brahmins advocating for social justice may become targets of political instrumentalization, with their actions being co-opted by political parties for partisan agendas. Political polarization and opportunism can undermine the authenticity and effectiveness of Brahmin-led social justice initiatives, turning them into tools for political gain rather than genuine efforts to address social inequalities.

6. Internal Critique and Accountability:

Brahmins engaged in social justice advocacy must also contend with internal critique and accountability within their own community. They may face scrutiny and pressure to reconcile their advocacy with the realities of Brahmin privilege and historical injustices. Balancing the need for introspection and accountability with external advocacy efforts poses a significant challenge for Brahmins committed to social justice.

Brahmins face numerous challenges and criticisms in their pursuit of social justice, ranging from historical legacies of privilege to contemporary prejudices and political dynamics. Overcoming these hurdles requires a nuanced approach that acknowledges Brahmin privilege while actively working towards dismantling caste-based hierarchies and promoting inclusivity. By addressing internal divisions, challenging stereotypes, and fostering genuine dialogue, Brahmins can play a meaningful role in advancing social justice and creating a more equitable society for all.

Chapter 17: The Brahmin and Globalization

In an era marked by interconnectedness and cultural exchange, the Brahmin community finds itself at the intersection of tradition and globalization. As custodians of ancient knowledge and spiritual heritage, Brahmins grapple with the challenges and opportunities presented by globalization, navigating a delicate balance between preserving their cultural identity and adapting to the forces of global change.

Globalization, characterized by increased interconnectedness and integration across borders, has brought about significant changes in various aspects of life, including culture, economy, and technology. For the Brahmin community, globalization poses both opportunities and challenges. On one hand, it provides avenues for the dissemination of traditional knowledge, spiritual teachings, and cultural practices to a global audience, fostering cross-cultural dialogue and appreciation. On the other hand, globalization also brings about the erosion of traditional values, the commodification of culture, and the homogenization of identities, raising concerns about cultural authenticity and preservation.

Against this backdrop, Brahmins grapple with questions of identity, authenticity, and adaptation in a globalized world. They navigate the complexities of preserving their cultural heritage while embracing the opportunities afforded by globalization.

From leveraging digital platforms to disseminate knowledge to engaging in cross-cultural exchanges and collaborations, Brahmins are actively shaping their role in an increasingly interconnected world. However, they also face challenges such as cultural appropriation, commodification of spiritual practices, and the dilution of traditional values in the face of globalized consumerism.

The relationship between Brahmins and globalization is multifaceted, reflecting a complex interplay between tradition and modernity. As globalization continues to reshape the cultural landscape, Brahmins find themselves at the forefront of preserving their heritage while engaging with the opportunities and challenges of a rapidly changing world. By striking a balance between tradition and innovation, Brahmins navigate the currents of globalization while upholding their cultural identity and values in an ever-evolving global context.

The impact of globalization on Brahmin culture and traditions

Globalization, with its interconnectedness and rapid exchange of ideas, goods, and people across borders, has significantly influenced Brahmin culture and traditions. This phenomenon has brought about both positive transformations and challenges for the Brahmin community, reshaping their identity, practices, and relationships in profound ways. Let's explore the impact of globalization on Brahmin culture and traditions in detail:

Cultural Exchange and Hybridization:

Globalization has facilitated cultural exchange between Brahmins and diverse communities worldwide. This exchange has led to the hybridization of Brahmin culture, as they incorporate elements from different traditions and adapt to multicultural environments. For example, Brahmins may adopt new dietary habits, clothing styles, or language influences from interactions with global cultures.

Digital Connectivity and Knowledge Dissemination: The advent of digital technology and the internet has enabled Brahmins to disseminate their cultural and spiritual knowledge globally. Online platforms provide avenues for sharing religious texts, philosophical teachings, and cultural practices with a wider audience, transcending geographical boundaries and reaching individuals from diverse backgrounds.

Commercialization and Consumerism:
Globalization has also led to the
commercialization of Brahmin culture, with
traditional practices and rituals often
commodified for commercial gain. This
trend raises concerns about the
authenticity and sanctity of cultural
traditions, as commercial interests
sometimes overshadow spiritual values.

Challenges to Traditional Values: The influx
of Western ideals and consumerist culture
has posed challenges to traditional Brahmin
values and ethics. Materialism,
individualism, and secularism may clash
with the emphasis on spiritual pursuits,
community welfare, and adherence to
moral principles traditionally upheld by
Brahmins.

Cultural Appropriation: Globalization has

exposed Brahmin culture to appropriation and misrepresentation, with elements of their religious practices and traditions often misunderstood or exploited for commercial or sensational purposes. This phenomenon raises awareness about the need to protect and preserve Brahmin cultural heritage from misappropriation and distortion.

Migration and Diaspora Communities: Globalization has led to increased migration of Brahmins to foreign countries, resulting in the formation of diaspora communities. These communities face unique challenges in maintaining cultural continuity while adapting to the cultural norms and practices of their host countries.

Globalization has had a profound impact on Brahmin culture and traditions, influencing their practices, beliefs, and interactions with the global community. While globalization has provided opportunities for cultural exchange and knowledge dissemination, it has also posed challenges such as commercialization, cultural appropriation, and the erosion of traditional values. Brahmins navigate these complexities by striving to preserve their cultural heritage while embracing the opportunities and confronting the challenges of a globalized world.

The challenges and opportunities for Brahmins in a globalized world

As globalization continues to reshape the cultural, economic, and social landscape, Brahmins find themselves navigating a complex array of challenges and opportunities. From preserving their cultural heritage to adapting to new realities, Brahmins confront a myriad of factors that shape their role in a globalized world. Let's delve into the specific challenges and opportunities they encounter:

Challenges:

Cultural Dilution: Globalization often leads to the dilution of traditional cultural practices as Brahmins are exposed to external influences. This dilution can erode cultural authenticity and challenge the preservation of traditional values and customs.

Cultural Appropriation: Brahmin culture may be subject to appropriation and misrepresentation by external entities, leading to distortion and misunderstanding of their religious beliefs, practices, and traditions.

Economic Disparities: Globalization can exacerbate economic disparities within Brahmin communities, as rapid economic changes and technological advancements may disproportionately benefit certain segments while marginalizing others.

Social Fragmentation: Increased mobility and interconnectedness may lead to social fragmentation within Brahmin communities, as individuals and families spread across different regions or countries face challenges in maintaining cohesive social networks and identity.

Identity Crisis: Brahmins may experience an identity crisis in a globalized world, as they grapple with the tension between preserving their cultural heritage and embracing modernity. This tension can lead to feelings of displacement and uncertainty about their place in an evolving society.

Opportunities:

Global Networking: Globalization provides Brahmins with opportunities to connect and collaborate with individuals and communities worldwide, fostering cross-cultural dialogue and exchange of ideas.

Educational Access: Improved access to education and information technology enables Brahmins to enhance their knowledge and skills, empowering them to adapt to changing economic and social landscapes.

Cultural Exchange: Globalization facilitates cultural exchange, allowing Brahmins to share their rich cultural heritage with a global audience and learn from diverse cultural traditions and practices.

Entrepreneurial Ventures: Brahmins can leverage globalization to explore entrepreneurial ventures and business opportunities, tapping into global markets and networks to promote economic growth and innovation.

Advocacy for Social Justice: Brahmins can use their global influence and networks to advocate for social justice, human rights, and environmental sustainability on a global scale, contributing to positive social change and collective well-being.

Brahmins face a complex array of challenges and opportunities in a globalized world. While globalization presents threats to cultural authenticity and social cohesion, it also offers avenues for cultural exchange, economic empowerment, and global advocacy. By navigating these challenges with resilience and adaptability, Brahmins can harness the opportunities presented by globalization to preserve their cultural heritage, promote social justice, and contribute to a more inclusive and interconnected world.

The efforts of Brahmins to preserve their identity and values in the face of globalization

Globalization has ushered in an era of unprecedented cultural exchange and interconnectedness, posing both opportunities and challenges for Brahmins in preserving their identity and values. In response to the forces of globalization, Brahmins have undertaken various efforts to safeguard their cultural heritage and uphold their traditional values. Let's explore these efforts in detail:

Cultural Revivalism: Brahmins have engaged in initiatives aimed at reviving and promoting traditional cultural practices, including religious rituals, linguistic traditions, and artistic expressions. These efforts involve organizing cultural festivals, preserving ancient manuscripts, and promoting classical arts such as music, dance, and literature.

Education and Knowledge Preservation:
Recognizing the importance of education in transmitting cultural heritage, Brahmins have focused on educating the younger generation about their traditions, scriptures, and values. This includes establishing educational institutions, conducting workshops, and fostering mentorship programs to impart traditional knowledge to future generations.

Community Engagement and Social Cohesion: Brahmins have emphasized community engagement and social cohesion as essential elements in preserving their identity amidst globalization. They organize community gatherings, social events, and religious ceremonies to foster solidarity and a sense of belonging among Brahmin communities, both locally and globally.

Advocacy for Cultural Preservation:
Brahmins actively advocate for policies and
initiatives that support the preservation of
their cultural heritage and traditions. They
engage with government agencies, cultural
organizations, and international bodies to
raise awareness about the importance of
preserving Brahmin culture and ensuring its
continued vitality in a globalized world.

Adaptation and Innovation: While
preserving traditional values, Brahmins also
recognize the need for adaptation and
innovation to thrive in a rapidly changing
global landscape. They embrace technology
and modern communication platforms to
disseminate cultural knowledge, connect
with global audiences, and adapt traditional
practices to contemporary contexts.

Promotion of Ethical Values: Brahmins

emphasize the importance of ethical values such as compassion, integrity, and humility in navigating the challenges of globalization. They promote ethical leadership, social responsibility, and sustainable living practices as integral aspects of their cultural identity and values.

Cross-Cultural Dialogue and Collaboration: Brahmins actively engage in cross-cultural dialogue and collaboration with diverse communities to foster mutual understanding, respect, and appreciation for cultural diversity. They participate in interfaith dialogues, cultural exchange programs, and collaborative projects that promote harmony and cooperation across cultural and religious boundaries.

Brahmins' efforts to preserve their identity and values in the face of globalization reflect their resilience, adaptability, and commitment to cultural heritage. By embracing both tradition and innovation, Brahmins navigate the complexities of globalization while safeguarding their cultural legacy for future generations. Through collective action, advocacy, and collaboration, Brahmins strive to ensure that their rich cultural heritage continues to flourish and inspire in an increasingly interconnected world.

Chapter 18: The Brahmin and Stereotypes

Stereotypes surrounding the Brahmin community have persisted for generations, often shaping perceptions and attitudes towards its members. These stereotypes, rooted in historical, social, and cultural contexts, have contributed to both positive and negative portrayals of Brahmins in society.

The Brahmin community, as custodians of ancient knowledge and spiritual traditions, has been both revered and vilified throughout history. While Brahmins are often portrayed as wise scholars, spiritual leaders, and guardians of tradition, they are also subjected to stereotypes that depict them as elitist, conservative, and disconnected from the realities of modern life. These stereotypes not only oversimplify the diverse experiences and identities within the Brahmin community but also contribute to misconceptions and prejudices that can perpetuate social divisions and inequality.

Through an exploration of Brahmin stereotypes, we aim to challenge preconceived notions, promote critical thinking, and foster greater understanding and empathy towards the Brahmin community. By interrogating the origins and implications of these stereotypes, we seek to pave the way for meaningful dialogue, reconciliation, and the dismantling of harmful stereotypes that hinder social cohesion and mutual respect.

Stereotypes are oversimplified, generalized beliefs about a particular group that may not accurately reflect the diversity and complexity of individuals within that group. The Brahmin community, like many other social groups, is subject to various stereotypes, some of which have persisted over time. Let's explore some common stereotypes associated with Brahmins:

Intellectual Elitism: One prevalent stereotype about Brahmins is their perceived intellectual elitism. They are often depicted as highly educated, scholarly individuals who occupy positions of authority in academia, religion, and other intellectual pursuits. While many Brahmins do excel in intellectual fields, this stereotype can overlook the diversity of educational backgrounds and interests within the community.

Cultural Conservatism: Brahmins are sometimes stereotyped as being culturally conservative, adhering strictly to traditional practices and values. This stereotype may portray them as resistant to change and innovation, particularly in matters of social and cultural evolution. While Brahmins do value tradition and heritage, this stereotype can overlook the community's capacity for adaptation and innovation.

Social Privilege: Another stereotype associated with Brahmins is their perceived social privilege and entitlement. They are often portrayed as belonging to the upper echelons of society, enjoying socio-economic advantages and opportunities not available to other groups. While historical factors may have contributed to Brahmins' social status in certain contexts, this stereotype can overlook the socio-economic diversity within the community and the challenges faced by many Brahmins.

Religious Orthodoxy: Brahmins are sometimes stereotyped as being religiously orthodox, rigidly adhering to traditional Hindu practices and beliefs. This stereotype may portray them as intolerant of other religious traditions and resistant to religious reform. While Brahmins do play a significant role in Hindu religious practices, this stereotype can overlook the diversity of religious beliefs and practices within the community.

Caste Discrimination: Brahmins are often

stereotyped as perpetrators of caste discrimination, particularly in the context of the historical caste system in India. They may be portrayed as upholding caste-based hierarchies and discriminating against lower-caste individuals. While historical injustices may have occurred, this stereotype can perpetuate prejudice and overlook efforts by many Brahmins to promote social justice and equality.

Stereotypes associated with Brahmins often oversimplify and distort the diverse realities of individuals within the community. While some stereotypes may contain elements of truth, they should be critically examined and not used to generalize or discriminate against Brahmins as a whole. Understanding the complexity of Brahmin identity and challenging stereotypes is essential for fostering mutual respect, empathy, and social inclusion.

Stereotypes, while often rooted in misconceptions and generalizations, can have profound and detrimental effects on the targeted group. For the Brahmin community, these stereotypes can perpetuate prejudice, discrimination, and marginalization, leading to a range of harmful consequences. Let's explore some of these effects in detail:

Social Stigma and Alienation: Stereotypes portraying Brahmins as elitist, privileged, or discriminatory can contribute to social stigma and alienation within society. Brahmins may face prejudice and discrimination based on these stereotypes, leading to exclusion from social, educational, and economic opportunities.

Psychological Impact: Constant exposure to negative stereotypes can have a detrimental impact on the psychological well-being of Brahmins. Internalizing stereotypes can lead to feelings of shame, inadequacy, and self-doubt, affecting their self-esteem and mental health. Brahmins may experience heightened stress, anxiety, and depression as a result of societal perceptions and expectations.

Interpersonal Conflict: Stereotypes can strain interpersonal relationships and interactions within Brahmin communities and with others. Misconceptions about Brahmins' beliefs, values, and behaviors may lead to misunderstandings, conflicts, and strained social dynamics. This can create barriers to communication and collaboration, hindering social cohesion and mutual understanding.

Educational and Professional Barriers:
Stereotypes about Brahmins' intellectual elitism or social privilege can create barriers to educational and professional advancement. Brahmin individuals may face prejudice and discrimination in educational institutions, workplaces, and other settings, limiting their opportunities for academic and career success.

Cultural Erasure and Misrepresentation:
Stereotypes may contribute to the erasure or misrepresentation of Brahmin culture and heritage. Simplistic portrayals of Brahmins in media, literature, and popular culture can perpetuate stereotypes and overlook the diversity and richness of Brahmin traditions, beliefs, and contributions to society.

Undermining Social Justice Efforts:
Stereotypes about Brahmins' role in

perpetuating caste discrimination can undermine efforts to promote social justice and equality. These stereotypes may divert attention from systemic inequalities and injustices faced by marginalized communities, hindering collective efforts to address caste-based discrimination and oppression.

Impact on Identity and Belonging:
Stereotypes can shape Brahmins' sense of identity and belonging within society. Negative stereotypes may lead Brahmins to question their place in society, cultural heritage, and community affiliations. This can contribute to feelings of isolation, identity crisis, and disconnection from their cultural roots.

The harmful effects of stereotypes on the Brahmin community are far-reaching and multifaceted, impacting individuals' social, psychological, and economic well-being. Addressing stereotypes requires challenging misconceptions, promoting empathy and understanding, and advocating for social justice and equality. By challenging stereotypes and fostering inclusivity, society can create a more equitable and respectful environment for all individuals, regardless of their background or identity.

The need to break these stereotypes and promote understanding and acceptance

Stereotypes surrounding the Brahmin community, like any form of prejudice, hinder societal progress and perpetuate discrimination and inequality. To foster a more inclusive and equitable society, it is imperative to break these stereotypes and promote understanding and acceptance of the Brahmin community. Here's why:

Fostering Empathy and Compassion: Breaking stereotypes requires cultivating empathy and compassion towards individuals from the Brahmin community. By recognizing the diversity and complexity of Brahmin identities and experiences, society can develop a deeper understanding of their perspectives, struggles, and contributions.

Challenging Misconceptions: Stereotypes often stem from ignorance and misinformation. By challenging misconceptions and providing accurate information about Brahmin culture, beliefs, and practices, society can debunk stereotypes and promote a more nuanced understanding of the community.

Promoting Social Cohesion: Stereotypes create divisions and barriers between different social groups, hindering social cohesion and unity. By breaking stereotypes and fostering mutual respect and acceptance, society can build stronger bonds and promote solidarity across diverse communities.

Ensuring Equal Opportunities: Stereotypes can perpetuate discrimination and limit opportunities for individuals from the Brahmin community in various spheres of life, including education, employment, and social interactions. By combating stereotypes, society can create a more level playing field where all individuals have equal access to opportunities and resources.

Creating Inclusive Spaces: Stereotypes can lead to exclusion and marginalization of

Brahmins from social, cultural, and institutional spaces. By challenging stereotypes and creating inclusive environments that celebrate diversity, society can ensure that Brahmins feel valued, respected, and included in all aspects of community life.

Promoting Cultural Appreciation: Breaking stereotypes involves promoting appreciation and respect for Brahmin culture, heritage, and contributions to society. By recognizing and celebrating Brahmin art, literature, science, and spirituality, society can foster a greater sense of cultural pride and appreciation for the community's rich cultural legacy.

Building Bridges of Understanding:
Breaking stereotypes requires building bridges of understanding and dialogue

between different social groups. By engaging in open and honest conversations, actively listening to diverse perspectives, and seeking common ground, society can foster mutual understanding and bridge divides between Brahmins and other communities.

Breaking stereotypes and promoting understanding and acceptance of the Brahmin community is essential for building a more inclusive, tolerant, and equitable society. It requires collective efforts from individuals, communities, institutions, and policymakers to challenge misconceptions, foster empathy, and create a society where all individuals are valued, respected, and given equal opportunities to thrive. By working together to break stereotypes, society can move closer towards realizing its ideals of justice, equality, and social harmony.

Chapter 19: The Brahmin and Social Media

In today's digital age, social media platforms have become powerful tools for communication, networking, and expression. For the Brahmin community, social media presents both opportunities and challenges in navigating virtual spaces while preserving cultural heritage and fostering community engagement.

Social media platforms offer Brahmins a platform to connect with fellow community members, share cultural insights, and celebrate traditions on a global scale. From Facebook groups dedicated to religious discourse to Instagram accounts showcasing artistic endeavors, social media has facilitated the exchange of ideas and experiences among Brahmins worldwide. Additionally, platforms like Twitter and LinkedIn enable Brahmins to engage in professional networking, share knowledge, and amplify their voices in various fields.

However, the proliferation of social media also poses challenges for the Brahmin community, including the spread of misinformation, cultural appropriation, and the erosion of traditional values in digital spaces. As Brahmins navigate the digital landscape, they must strike a balance between embracing technological advancements and preserving cultural authenticity. Through critical engagement, ethical use of social media, and community collaboration, Brahmins can harness the potential of digital platforms to promote cultural awareness, foster dialogue, and strengthen bonds within their community.

The impact of social media on Brahmin community

Social media has revolutionized how individuals interact, communicate, and engage with information in the digital age. For the Brahmin community, social media platforms have had a multifaceted impact, shaping cultural expression, community engagement, and identity formation. Let's delve into the various dimensions of this impact:

Cultural Visibility and Promotion: Social media platforms provide Brahmins with a global stage to showcase their cultural heritage, traditions, and practices. Through platforms like Instagram, YouTube, and Facebook, Brahmins can share videos, photos, and posts that celebrate festivals, rituals, and artistic expressions. This increased visibility helps promote awareness and appreciation of Brahmin culture among a wider audience.

Community Building and Networking:
Social media facilitates virtual community building among Brahmins, enabling individuals from diverse geographical locations to connect, interact, and collaborate. Brahmin-specific groups and forums on platforms like WhatsApp and LinkedIn serve as spaces for networking, knowledge sharing, and mutual support. These digital communities foster a sense of belonging and solidarity among Brahmins worldwide.

Educational Resources and Discourse:

Social media platforms serve as repositories of educational resources, discussions, and debates on various topics relevant to the Brahmin community. Brahmin scholars, pundits, and educators use platforms like Twitter and YouTube to share insights on religious scriptures, philosophical teachings, and cultural practices. This democratization of knowledge enhances access to learning opportunities and promotes intellectual engagement within the community.

Challenges of Misinformation and Cultural Appropriation: Despite its benefits, social media also presents challenges for the Brahmin community, including the proliferation of misinformation and cultural appropriation. Misinterpretation of religious texts, distortion of cultural practices, and misrepresentation of Brahmin identity are common occurrences on digital platforms. Additionally, cultural elements such as rituals, attire, and symbols may be appropriated or commodified without proper understanding or respect for their significance.

Identity Negotiation and Representation: Social media platforms influence how Brahmins perceive and present their identity in the digital realm. Individuals may curate their online persona to reflect aspects of Brahmin identity, such as religious affiliations, professional achievements, or cultural interests. However, navigating digital spaces also requires negotiating issues of authenticity, privacy, and representation, as Brahmins balance their online presence with offline realities.

Engagement with Social Issues: Social media serves as a platform for Brahmins to engage with social issues, advocate for causes, and participate in public discourse. From discussions on caste discrimination to campaigns for social justice, Brahmins use platforms like Twitter, Instagram, and Facebook to raise awareness and mobilize support for various social causes. This digital activism amplifies Brahmins' voices and contributes to broader conversations on equity and inclusion.

Social media has profoundly influenced the Brahmin community's engagement with culture, community, and identity. While it offers opportunities for cultural promotion, community building, and intellectual discourse, it also presents challenges related to misinformation, appropriation, and identity representation. By navigating these complexities with critical awareness and ethical engagement, Brahmins can harness the transformative potential of social media while preserving the integrity of their cultural heritage and values.

The role of social media in perpetuating stereotypes and misconceptions about Brahmins

Social media, with its vast reach and instantaneous dissemination of information, plays a significant role in shaping public perceptions and narratives about different social groups. Unfortunately, for the Brahmin community, social media has often served as a platform for the perpetuation of stereotypes and misconceptions. Let's delve into the various ways in which social media contributes to this phenomenon:

Amplification of Negative Narratives: Social media platforms amplify negative narratives and stereotypes about Brahmins through the rapid sharing of content. Misleading or sensationalized posts that depict Brahmins in a negative light can quickly go viral, reinforcing pre-existing biases and misconceptions among users.

Selective Representation: Social media users often cherry-pick and highlight instances that conform to existing stereotypes about Brahmins while ignoring or downplaying counter-narratives. This selective representation distorts reality and perpetuates one-dimensional portrayals of the Brahmin community, reinforcing stereotypes in the process.

Echo Chambers and Confirmation Bias: Social media algorithms tend to create echo chambers where users are exposed to content that aligns with their existing beliefs and biases. This can lead to confirmation bias, where users selectively consume and share content that confirms their negative perceptions of Brahmins, further entrenching stereotypes within online communities.

Misinformation Campaigns: Social media platforms are vulnerable to misinformation campaigns that target specific communities, including Brahmins. False or misleading information about Brahmin culture, history, and practices can be disseminated widely, leading to the perpetuation of stereotypes and misconceptions among a broader audience.

Viral Memes and Satirical Content: Memes and satirical content shared on social media often rely on stereotypes for humor or entertainment value. While intended as lighthearted humor, these memes can reinforce negative stereotypes about Brahmins and contribute to the normalization of discriminatory attitudes towards the community.

Cyberbullying and Online Harassment: Brahmins may also face cyberbullying and online harassment based on their caste identity. Social media platforms provide anonymity to perpetrators, enabling them to target individuals from the Brahmin community with derogatory comments, hate speech, and threats, further marginalizing and stigmatizing the community.

Lack of Counter-Narratives: Despite efforts by some Brahmins to challenge stereotypes and promote accurate representations of their community on social media, these counter-narratives often struggle to gain traction amidst the flood of sensationalized or biased content. As a result, stereotypes and misconceptions continue to dominate online discourse.

Social media plays a pivotal role in perpetuating stereotypes and misconceptions about Brahmins through the amplification of negative narratives, selective representation, confirmation bias, misinformation campaigns, viral content, cyberbullying, and the lack of counter-narratives. Addressing this issue requires concerted efforts from platform administrators, content creators, and users to promote accuracy, empathy, and cultural sensitivity in online interactions. By challenging stereotypes and fostering informed dialogue, social media can become a more inclusive and respectful space for all communities, including

Brahmins.

The efforts of Brahmins to use social media to promote their culture and values

In response to the perpetuation of stereotypes and misconceptions about their community on social media, Brahmins have increasingly leveraged digital platforms to promote their culture, values, and contributions. These efforts encompass a range of initiatives aimed at fostering awareness, fostering dialogue, and countering negative narratives. Let's delve into the various ways in which Brahmins are using social media to promote their culture and values:

Educational Content Creation: Brahmins

are actively creating and sharing educational content on social media platforms to provide accurate insights into their culture, traditions, and history. This includes informative videos, articles, and infographics that debunk stereotypes, clarify misconceptions, and highlight the diverse aspects of Brahmin identity and heritage.

Cultural Celebrations and Festivals:
Brahmins utilize social media to showcase their cultural celebrations, festivals, and rituals, providing glimpses into their rich cultural heritage. Through photos, videos, and live streams, Brahmins share the significance of various traditions, fostering appreciation and understanding among a wider audience.

Promotion of Art, Music, and Literature:
Brahmins are active contributors to art, music, literature, and other creative endeavors, which they promote through social media platforms. They share their artistic creations, performances, and literary works, enriching the digital landscape with their cultural expressions and talents.

Dialogue and Advocacy: Brahmins engage in online dialogue and advocacy to address stereotypes, challenge discrimination, and promote social justice. They participate in discussions, forums, and campaigns on social media platforms to raise awareness about issues affecting their community and advocate for positive change.

Networking and Community Building:
Brahmins use social media for networking

and community building, connecting with fellow community members and organizations worldwide. Platforms like Facebook, LinkedIn, and Twitter serve as spaces for Brahmins to exchange ideas, collaborate on initiatives, and support each other professionally and personally.

Empowerment and Representation: Social media provides Brahmins with a platform to amplify their voices, share their stories, and assert their identity in the digital realm. By showcasing their achievements, contributions, and aspirations, Brahmins strive to reclaim agency and representation in online spaces.

Educational Campaigns and Workshops: Brahmins organize educational campaigns, workshops, and webinars on social media platforms to promote cultural literacy, foster intercultural dialogue, and combat stereotypes. These initiatives aim to educate both Brahmins and non-Brahmins about the complexities of Brahmin identity and heritage.

Brahmins are actively utilizing social media as a tool for cultural promotion, value advocacy, and community empowerment. Through educational content creation, cultural celebrations, promotion of artistic endeavors, dialogue and advocacy, networking, empowerment, and educational campaigns, Brahmins are reshaping online narratives and fostering a more nuanced understanding of their community. These efforts contribute to building bridges of understanding, fostering inclusivity, and promoting cultural pride among Brahmins and the broader society.

Chapter 20: The Brahmin and Cultural Appropriation

Cultural appropriation, the adoption or use of elements of one culture by members of another culture without permission or understanding, has become a contentious issue in today's globalized world. For the Brahmin community, cultural appropriation presents unique challenges and considerations due to the rich and diverse cultural heritage associated with their identity.

Brahmins, as custodians of ancient traditions, rituals, art forms, and knowledge systems, have long grappled with the appropriation of their cultural heritage by external entities. From misrepresentation of religious practices to commodification of traditional attire and symbols, Brahmins have witnessed the misappropriation of their cultural identity on various fronts. This phenomenon not only erodes the authenticity and integrity of Brahmin culture but also perpetuates stereotypes and misconceptions about the community.

As Brahmins navigate the complexities of cultural appropriation, they confront questions of authenticity, ownership, and respect for cultural heritage. Through dialogue, advocacy, and creative expression, Brahmins seek to reclaim agency over their cultural narrative and foster greater awareness and appreciation of their traditions.

Cultural appropriation refers to the adoption or use of elements from one culture by individuals or groups outside of that culture, often without proper understanding, acknowledgment, or respect for its significance. For the Brahmin community, which boasts a rich tapestry of cultural heritage encompassing religious practices, rituals, art forms, and knowledge systems, cultural appropriation has profound implications. Let's delve into the concept of cultural appropriation and its impact on Brahmin culture:

Misrepresentation of Religious Practices: One significant impact of cultural appropriation on Brahmin culture is the misrepresentation of religious practices.

Sacred rituals, ceremonies, and spiritual beliefs integral to Brahmin identity may be distorted, simplified, or sensationalized when appropriated by external entities. This misrepresentation not only dilutes the authenticity of Brahmin religious traditions but also perpetuates misconceptions and stereotypes about the community.

Commodification of Cultural Symbols: Cultural appropriation often leads to the commodification of Brahmin cultural symbols, such as religious artifacts, attire, and symbols. These symbols, imbued with deep spiritual and cultural significance, may be commercialized for profit or used out of context, diminishing their sacredness and cultural value. This commodification reduces Brahmin culture to mere commodities, eroding its integrity and authenticity.

Erosion of Traditional Knowledge Systems: Brahmins have historically served as repositories of ancient knowledge systems, including Vedic texts, Sanskrit literature, and scientific advancements. However, cultural appropriation can lead to the exploitation and extraction of this knowledge without proper acknowledgment or understanding of its origins. As a result, Brahmin contributions to intellectual and scientific advancements may be overlooked or appropriated by other cultures, diminishing Brahmin cultural heritage.

Reinforcement of Stereotypes: Cultural appropriation reinforces stereotypes and misconceptions about the Brahmin community, perpetuating harmful narratives that essentialize and homogenize Brahmin identity. External appropriation often reduces Brahmins to caricatures or exoticized figures, overlooking the diversity and complexity of their cultural heritage. This reinforcement of stereotypes further marginalizes Brahmins and undermines their agency in defining their cultural identity.

Loss of Cultural Sovereignty: Cultural appropriation threatens the sovereignty of Brahmin culture by diminishing Brahmins' authority over their own cultural narrative and practices. When elements of Brahmin culture are appropriated without consent or understanding, Brahmins lose control over how their traditions are represented and interpreted, leading to a loss of cultural autonomy and agency.

Cultural appropriation has far-reaching implications for Brahmin culture, impacting religious practices, cultural symbols, traditional knowledge systems, stereotypes, and cultural sovereignty. As Brahmins navigate the complexities of cultural appropriation, they strive to assert agency over their cultural narrative, advocate for respect and recognition of their traditions, and foster greater awareness and appreciation of their rich cultural heritage. Through dialogue, education, and advocacy, Brahmins endeavor to preserve and protect their cultural identity in the face of appropriation and exploitation.

The instances of cultural appropriation of Brahmin traditions and practices

Cultural appropriation of Brahmin traditions and practices occurs when elements of Brahmin culture are adopted, misrepresented, or exploited by individuals or groups outside the community, often without proper understanding or acknowledgment of their significance. Here are several instances of cultural appropriation of Brahmin traditions and practices:

Misrepresentation of Religious Rituals:
One common form of cultural appropriation involves the misrepresentation of Brahmin religious rituals. Sacred ceremonies such as Yagnas (fire rituals), Puja (worship), and Samskaras (sacraments) are often depicted inaccurately or sensationalized in mainstream media or popular culture, reducing complex spiritual practices to superficial portrayals.

Commercialization of Traditional Attire:
Traditional Brahmin attire, such as the dhoti, kurta, and janeu (sacred thread), has been commodified and appropriated by

fashion designers and brands for profit. These garments, imbued with cultural and religious significance, are often stripped of their sacredness and reduced to mere fashion statements, devoid of their original context and meaning.

Use of Sanskrit Mantras and Symbols:
Sanskrit mantras, symbols, and verses from ancient texts such as the Vedas and Upanishads are frequently appropriated and used out of context by individuals or groups for commercial or recreational purposes. These sacred elements, intended for spiritual contemplation and worship, are often trivialized or distorted when appropriated without proper reverence or understanding.

Adoption of Yoga and Meditation Practices: The widespread popularity of yoga and meditation in Western countries has led to the appropriation of these practices from their Brahmin origins. While yoga and meditation offer numerous physical and mental health benefits, their commercialization and secularization often overlook their spiritual roots and cultural significance within Brahmin tradition.

Cultural Fusion in Cuisine: Hindu cuisine, known for its vegetarian and sattvic (pure) principles, has been appropriated and adapted in fusion cuisines without acknowledgment of its Brahmin origins. Dishes such as masala dosa, idli, and sambar, originally part of Brahmin culinary traditions, are now popularized and commercialized as generic "Indian" cuisine without recognition of their cultural heritage.

New Age Spiritual Practices: New age spiritual movements often appropriate elements of Hindu spirituality, such as meditation techniques, mantra chanting, and Ayurvedic principles, while divorcing them from their cultural and philosophical foundations. This appropriation can lead to the dilution or distortion of traditional Brahmin spiritual practices and philosophies.

Commercialization of Festivals: Hindu festivals and celebrations, such as Diwali, Navaratri, and Janmashtami, are increasingly commercialized and appropriated for commercial purposes. Corporate entities may capitalize on these festivals through sales promotions, marketing campaigns, and branding strategies, often diluting their spiritual and cultural significance in the process.

These instances of cultural appropriation highlight the complexities and challenges faced by the Brahmin community in safeguarding their cultural heritage from exploitation and misrepresentation. As Brahmins navigate the impact of cultural appropriation, they strive to raise awareness, advocate for respectful engagement with their traditions, and reclaim agency over their cultural narrative.

The need to respect and preserve Brahmin culture and traditions

Brahmin culture and traditions represent a rich tapestry of heritage, spirituality, and knowledge that have evolved over millennia. As custodians of ancient wisdom and guardians of sacred rituals, Brahmins play a pivotal role in preserving and transmitting cultural legacies from one generation to the next. Here's an exploration of the critical need to respect and preserve Brahmin culture and traditions:

Cultural Diversity and Pluralism: Brahmin culture contributes to the vibrant tapestry of Indian cultural diversity. Each aspect of Brahmin tradition, from religious practices to culinary arts, reflects the unique ethos and heritage of the community. Preserving Brahmin culture ensures the continuation of this rich diversity, enriching the cultural landscape of India and the world.

Historical Continuity: Brahmin culture embodies centuries-old traditions, rituals, and knowledge systems passed down through oral and written traditions. Preserving these cultural artifacts ensures the continuity of historical narratives and fosters a sense of connection to ancestral roots among Brahmins and future generations.

Spiritual and Philosophical Wisdom: Brahmin culture encompasses profound spiritual and philosophical insights embedded in Vedic texts, scriptures, and philosophical treatises. These teachings offer timeless wisdom on ethics, morality, and the pursuit of higher truths. Respecting and preserving Brahmin traditions allows for the dissemination of spiritual knowledge and fosters spiritual growth and introspection.

Social Cohesion and Harmony: Brahmin culture promotes values such as compassion, humility, and social responsibility, which are essential for fostering harmony and unity within society.

By upholding these values, Brahmins contribute to the promotion of social cohesion, tolerance, and mutual respect among diverse communities.

Cultural Heritage Conservation: Brahmin culture serves as a repository of intangible cultural heritage, including language, music, dance, and culinary arts. Preserving these cultural expressions safeguards against their erosion or extinction, ensuring their continued appreciation and enjoyment by future generations.

Intellectual Legacy: Brahmins have made significant contributions to various fields, including science, literature, philosophy, and the arts. By respecting and preserving Brahmin culture, society acknowledges and honors these intellectual contributions, fostering an environment conducive to further innovation and creative expression.

Promotion of Cultural Understanding:
Respecting Brahmin culture and traditions fosters intercultural understanding and appreciation, bridging gaps of misunderstanding and fostering dialogue among diverse communities. Through mutual respect and recognition, society can cultivate a deeper understanding of Brahmin heritage and its significance within the broader cultural tapestry.

The preservation and respect for Brahmin culture and traditions are essential for nurturing cultural diversity, historical continuity, spiritual wisdom, social cohesion, and intellectual legacy. By recognizing the value of Brahmin heritage and upholding its traditions, society honors the contributions of Brahmins to civilization

and ensures the enrichment of cultural life
for generations to come.

Chapter 21: Reflections

Understanding and appreciating the role of Brahmins in society is crucial for fostering a holistic perspective on cultural, spiritual, and intellectual contributions. Here's a detailed exploration of why acknowledging the role of Brahmins is important:

Preservation of Cultural Heritage:
Brahmins have been custodians of India's ancient cultural heritage for centuries. Their knowledge of Vedic scriptures, rituals, arts, and sciences has been instrumental in preserving and transmitting cultural traditions from generation to generation. Recognizing the role of Brahmins helps in safeguarding and promoting these

invaluable aspects of India's cultural legacy.

Promotion of Spiritual Wisdom: Brahmins have played a pivotal role in propagating spiritual wisdom and philosophical insights embedded in Hindu scriptures. Their teachings on ethics, morality, and spirituality have guided individuals on the path of self-realization and enlightenment. By appreciating the role of Brahmins, society gains access to profound spiritual knowledge that can inspire personal growth and introspection.

Intellectual Contributions: Brahmins have made significant contributions to various intellectual fields, including philosophy, literature, science, and mathematics. Scholars and thinkers from the Brahmin community have produced timeless works that have enriched human knowledge and understanding. Acknowledging these contributions fosters appreciation for Brahmin intellect and encourages the pursuit of knowledge and innovation.

Promotion of Social Welfare: Brahmins have historically played a role in promoting social welfare and community development. Through their involvement in education, charity, and religious institutions, Brahmins have contributed to the upliftment of marginalized communities and the provision of social services. Understanding their role in social welfare initiatives encourages collaborative efforts towards building a more equitable society.

Cultural Harmony and Diversity: Brahmins represent one of the many diverse cultural groups within India, each contributing to the country's cultural mosaic. Recognizing the role of Brahmins in preserving and promoting their unique cultural heritage fosters an environment of cultural harmony and mutual respect. Embracing cultural diversity strengthens social cohesion and enriches the collective tapestry of society.

Challenging Stereotypes: Appreciating the multifaceted role of Brahmins helps challenge stereotypes and misconceptions that may exist about the community. By acknowledging the diversity of experiences and contributions within the Brahmin community, society can move beyond simplistic generalizations and promote inclusivity and understanding.

Understanding and appreciating the role of Brahmins in society is essential for recognizing the richness of India's cultural and intellectual heritage, promoting spiritual wisdom, fostering social welfare, embracing cultural diversity, and challenging stereotypes. By valuing the contributions of Brahmins, society can cultivate a more inclusive and enlightened worldview that honors the diversity and complexity of human experience.

The need to break stereotypes and promote inclusivity and acceptance

Breaking stereotypes and promoting inclusivity and acceptance are imperative for fostering a more equitable, harmonious, and understanding society. Here's an in-depth exploration of the need to break stereotypes and advance inclusivity and acceptance:

Combatting Prejudice and Discrimination: Stereotypes often stem from prejudiced beliefs and misconceptions about particular groups or communities. These stereotypes can lead to discrimination, marginalization, and social exclusion. By actively challenging and dismantling stereotypes, society can mitigate the harmful effects of prejudice and promote equal treatment and opportunities for all individuals, regardless of their background.

Fostering Cultural Understanding:
Stereotypes arise from oversimplified and often distorted perceptions of different cultures, religions, or ethnicities. By breaking stereotypes, society can foster a deeper understanding and appreciation of diverse cultures, traditions, and worldviews. This understanding promotes cultural empathy, respect, and cooperation, leading to greater harmony and collaboration among individuals and communities.

Promoting Individuality and Diversity:
Stereotypes often overlook the individuality and diversity within communities, reducing people to one-dimensional caricatures based on superficial characteristics. Breaking stereotypes involves recognizing and celebrating the unique identities, experiences, and contributions of individuals from all backgrounds. Embracing diversity enriches society by bringing together a wide range of perspectives, talents, and strengths.

Creating Inclusive Spaces: Stereotypes can create barriers to inclusivity by perpetuating harmful assumptions and biases. To promote inclusivity, it is essential to create spaces and environments that welcome and value diversity. This includes workplaces, educational institutions, public spaces, and social platforms where individuals feel respected, empowered, and able to express their authentic selves without fear of judgment or discrimination.

Empowering Marginalized Groups:
Stereotypes often target marginalized or underrepresented groups, reinforcing systemic inequalities and power imbalances. By challenging stereotypes and promoting inclusivity, society can empower marginalized communities to assert their rights, amplify their voices, and participate fully in social, economic, and political life. This empowerment contributes to greater equity and social justice for all members of society.

Building Bridges Across Differences:
Stereotypes create divisions and foster

distrust among different groups within society. Breaking stereotypes and promoting inclusivity involve building bridges across cultural, religious, racial, and socioeconomic differences. By fostering meaningful connections and dialogue, society can cultivate empathy, understanding, and solidarity, leading to greater social cohesion and collective action towards shared goals.

Encouraging Critical Thinking: Breaking stereotypes requires individuals to critically examine their own biases and assumptions, as well as the broader narratives perpetuated by media, education, and popular culture. Encouraging critical thinking skills empowers individuals to question stereotypes, challenge misinformation, and engage in constructive dialogue that promotes inclusivity, acceptance, and mutual respect.

Breaking stereotypes and promoting inclusivity and acceptance are essential for fostering a more just, compassionate, and interconnected society. By challenging stereotypes, embracing diversity, and creating inclusive spaces, society can move towards a future where all individuals are valued, respected, and empowered to thrive.

The future of Brahmins and their contributions to society.

The future of Brahmins holds promise as they continue to make significant contributions to society across various fields. Here's an elaborate exploration of the future trajectory of Brahmins and their potential contributions:

Intellectual Advancements: Brahmins have historically been at the forefront of intellectual pursuits, making notable contributions to fields such as science, literature, philosophy, and technology. In the future, Brahmin scholars and thinkers are expected to continue pushing the boundaries of knowledge and innovation, driving advancements in diverse domains and shaping the intellectual landscape of society.

Cultural Preservation: Brahmins play a crucial role in preserving and promoting India's rich cultural heritage. With a deep-rooted understanding of Vedic traditions, classical arts, and religious practices, Brahmins are poised to safeguard cultural legacies for future generations. Their efforts in cultural preservation will help maintain the vibrancy and authenticity of Indian cultural traditions amidst globalization and modernization.

Social Advocacy: Brahmins have historically been advocates for social welfare and justice, leveraging their influence to address societal inequalities and injustices. In the future, Brahmins are likely to continue advocating for marginalized communities, promoting social inclusion, and striving towards a more equitable society. Their contributions to social advocacy will be instrumental in fostering greater harmony and solidarity within diverse communities.

Educational Leadership: Brahmins have traditionally been associated with education and scholarly pursuits, occupying roles as teachers, mentors, and educators. In the future, Brahmins are expected to play a significant role in educational leadership, shaping curricula, pedagogical approaches, and educational policies. Their commitment to knowledge dissemination and academic excellence will contribute to the advancement of education at all levels.

Entrepreneurship and Innovation: Brahmins have demonstrated entrepreneurial acumen and innovative thinking, contributing to economic development and job creation. In the future, Brahmin entrepreneurs are poised to drive innovation across sectors, from technology and finance to arts and crafts. Their entrepreneurial ventures will stimulate economic growth, foster creativity, and generate opportunities for societal advancement.

Spiritual Guidance: Brahmins have traditionally served as spiritual guides and mentors, offering insights into the realms of spirituality, ethics, and morality. In the future, Brahmin spiritual leaders are expected to continue providing guidance and support to individuals seeking spiritual fulfillment and moral direction. Their teachings will inspire personal growth, ethical conduct, and inner peace in an increasingly complex world.

Global Engagement: Brahmins are increasingly engaging with global communities, sharing their knowledge, cultural heritage, and values on international platforms. In the future, Brahmins will continue to participate in global dialogues, collaborations, and initiatives, contributing to cross-cultural understanding, peacebuilding, and global cooperation. Their global engagement will enrich the global community with diverse perspectives and insights from ancient wisdom traditions.

The future of Brahmins is characterized by a commitment to excellence, social responsibility, cultural preservation, and global engagement. As custodians of India's rich heritage and agents of positive change, Brahmins will continue to shape the trajectory of society, contributing to its progress and prosperity in the years to come.

www.ingramcontent.com/pod-product-compliance
Lightning Source LLC
Chambersburg PA
CBHW050313160726
48002CB00001B/20